English Grammar

Vocabulary, and Spelling Test Skills

- Gloria F. Williams -

Contents

1 Grammar Skills

1. What's the Infinitive…?
2. Troubling Tenses – Past Simple vs. Present Continuous 1
3. Troubling Tenses – Past Simple vs. Present Continuous 2
4. Troubling Tenses – Past Simple vs. 'going to' 1
5. Troubling Tenses – Past Simple vs. 'going to' 2
6. Troubling Tenses – Mixed Tenses 1
7. Troubling Tenses – Mixed Tenses 2
8. The Funny Noise – Irregular Verbs in the Past Simple Tense
9. Using Conjunctions – Mix & Match Cards 1
10. Using Conjunctions – Mix & Match Cards 2
11. Singular and Plural Nouns 1
12. Singular and Plural Nouns 2
13. Using Determiners 1
14. Using Determiners 2
15. Using Determiners 3

16 Vocabulary Skills

16. The Joy of Abstract Nouns 1
17. The Joy of Abstract Nouns 2
18. Emotions and Feelings 1
19. Emotions and Feelings 2
20. Common Idioms 1
21. Common Idioms 2
22. Understanding Quantities 1
23. Understanding Quantities 2
24. Shopping List – Mixed-up Quantities
25. Family Matters (gap-fill) 1
26. Family Matters (gap-fill) 2
27. My Relatives
28. Word Pyramid – Parts of a Sentence
29. Adjectives and Synonyms 1
30. Adjectives and Synonyms 2
31. Advanced Homophones 1
32. Advanced Homophones 2
33. Onomatopoeia – List of Noisy Words
34. Onomatopoeia – Noisy Words
35. Talking about the Weather 1
36. Talking about the Weather 2

37 Spelling Skills

37   100 Commonly Misspelled Words
38   Be the Spell-checker 1 – Going on Holiday
39   Be the Spell-checker 2 – Shopping List
40   Be the Spell-checker 3 – Giving Directions
41   Be the Spell-checker 4 – School Days
42   A Letter to Aunt Monica
43   Advanced Spelling Challenge 1
44   Advanced Spelling Challenge 2
45   Advanced Spelling Challenge 3
46   Advanced Spelling Challenge 4
47   Seeing the Sights in London

48 Reading Skills

48   Any Answers 1
49   Any Answers 2
50   Any Answers 3
51   Any Answers 4
52   Any Answers 5
53   Reading Comprehension 1 – Bob Hunter's Family
54   Reading Comprehension 2 – The Car Thief
55   Reading Comprehension 3 – A Lazy Holiday or an Exciting Holiday?
56   Reading Comprehension 4 – What Shall We Do Tomorrow?
57   Reading Comprehension 5 – Looking for a Job
58   Reading Comprehension 6 – How Much Money Do They Have?
59   Reading Comprehension 7 – When's Your Birthday?
60   Reading Comprehension 8 – Checking Train Times
61   Reading Comprehension 9 – First Day in Class
62   Reading Comprehension 10 – What's the Right Time?

63 Speaking & Listening Skills

63   Class Survey Template
64   A Fair Price?
65   Talking about a Picture or Object

66 Research Skills

66   Quick Quiz 1
67   Quick Quiz 2
68   Quick Quiz Template

69	Alphabet Quiz 1
70	Alphabet Quiz 2
71	Alphabet Quiz 3
72	Wordsearch Fun
73	Design a Board Game
74	Interesting Place Names 1
75	Interesting Place Names 2
76	Classic Books 1
77	Classic Books 2
78	The Life of Charles Dickens
79	An A-Z of English Slang Terms – Part 1
80	An A-Z of English Slang Terms – Part 2
81	Australian English Slang Terms – Part 1
82	Australian English Slang Terms – Part 2
83	Famous Quotations
84	Holidays and Special Days in the UK
85	Bingo Game Cards

86 Games for the Classroom

Speaking & Listening Skills

86	I-Spy
	Class Secrets
	Simon Says
	Party Invitations
	Something's Different
	Whispering Trees
87	What's Going On…?
	My Butler Went To Meadowhall
	What's In The Bag…?
	The Yes/No Game
88	Audio Pictures
	Our Living Photo Album

Reading and Writing Skills

	Ace Anagrams
	Hangman
	What Time Is It On…?
89	Board Game Boffins
	Ten Things
	What Shops Sell What…?

Vocabulary Building

Name And Explain

90 What Is It…?
What Am I…?

Grammar Skills

A Capital Game
Interesting Articles
The Instant Story Generator

Action Games

91 Balloon Rodins
Dead Heat
Get A Move On

92 Rhyming Words
International Phonetic Alphabet (IPA) – vowels and diphthongs

102 Answers to Worksheets and Notes for Use

Test Your Grammar Skills

What's the Infinitive...?

*The infinitive is the **basic form of a verb**.*

1. Underline the verb(s) in each sentence below.
2. Write the infinitive form of the verb(s) next to the sentence:

For example: I <u>went</u> shopping yesterday.   GO

1. What's her name?   _____
2. I don't know him.   _____
3. He went out.   _____
4. Are you watching TV?   _____
5. I saw him yesterday.   _____
6. I have brought my friend   _____
7. They lost some money.   _____
8. I don't like him.   _____
9. I have read your letter.   _____
10. We aren't learning much.   _____
11. I played on the computer.   _____
12. I couldn't hear you.   _____
13. Is it true?   _____
14. Did she tell you my name?   _____
15. That's her sister.   _____
16. The time was about 8pm.   _____
17. My arm really hurts.   _____
18. The children were laughing.   _____
19. I washed my hands.   _____
20. We're seeing them later.   _____

Troubling Tenses – Past Simple vs. Present Continuous 1

A. Complete each sentence using either **yesterday** or **tomorrow**:

1. I went to the cinema _____.

2. I'm playing golf _____.

3. We had an early lunch _____.

4. Her sister is going into hospital _____.

5. What time are you getting up _____?

6. I'm taking the car to the garage first thing _____.

7. My brother moved house _____.

8. Did you see that new music shop in town _____?

9. I met Lisa and Isabella for a coffee _____.

10. He's visiting his friend _____ afternoon.

11. There was a lot of noise outside _____.

12. We're going swimming _____ morning.

13. Are you coming round _____ evening?

14. He wasn't at work _____ afternoon because he went to hospital for an appointment.

15. John was in Birmingham all day _____ for a meeting.

B. Underline the main verb/s in each sentence (including compound verbs).

C. If the sentence contains an auxiliary verb (helping verb), circle it.

Troubling Tenses – Past Simple vs. Present Continuous 2

A. *Complete each sentence using either **yesterday** or **tomorrow**:*

1. I gave them some homework _____.

2. I'm not going on holiday until _____.

3. I missed the last bus _____, so I had to walk home.

4. It was cold _____, wasn't it?

5. Sally is getting her exam results _____.

6. We packed our suitcases _____ evening.

7. Is he still cooking lunch for his girlfriend and her family _____?

8. Bob and Janet are coming round for a game of cards _____ night.

9. We're flying to Spain _____ afternoon.

10. He's playing football for a couple of hours _____ morning.

11. I saw your friend Ian in Sainsbury's _____.

12. I'm doing all my ironing _____.

13. We both bought the same pair of shoes _____.

14. Is he going to tell you about the course _____, or later on today?

15. Jen swam forty lengths of the pool _____.

B. *Underline the main verb/s in each sentence (including compound verbs).*

C. *If the sentence contains an auxiliary verb (helping verb), circle it.*

Troubling Tenses – Past Simple vs. 'going to' 1

*Complete each sentence using either **yesterday** or **tomorrow**:*

1. I'm going to visit my sister _____ afternoon.

2. I went to my friend's house after work _____ evening.

3. The cricket match started at 2pm _____ afternoon.

4. I'm not going to play golf _____. I had a good game _____.

5. We're going to buy a present for our friend _____.

6. Rita told me _____ that she's going to quit her job.

7. I watched that film you told me about _____. It was brilliant.

8. Are you going to get some more potatoes _____?

9. She got up at quarter to ten _____ morning!

10. She's going to get up earlier _____ morning.

11. I'm going to book a restaurant first thing _____.

12. He was really tired _____, so he stayed at home all day.

13. I saw Ben _____. He's going to call you _____ night.

14. I finished reading that book you lent me _____.

15. Are you going to leave _____ or on Monday?

4.

Troubling Tenses – Past Simple vs. 'going to' 2

*Complete each sentence using either **yesterday** or **tomorrow**:*

1. Phil's going to meet Abdul in town _____ afternoon.

2. Sereta didn't look very happy when I saw her _____.

3. We didn't get our exam results _____ as promised.

4. Is James going to go on the trip _____?

5. The builders finished early _____; at about 5 o'clock.

6. Sarah and Natalie are going to travel to London _____.

7. Are you going to see that new Mel Gibson film when it comes out _____?

8. Did you watch the news _____?

9. You're going to feel tired _____ after all that exercise!

10. Did you send me an email _____?

11. I'm going to wash the car _____.

12. Because my sister fell out with her best friend _____, they're not going to the gig _____ night.

13. Pete said he's going to walk to work _____.

14. _____, Olivier said that he isn't going to come to class next week because it's his granddad's birthday on Monday.

15. Were you at home _____ evening?

Troubling Tenses – Mixed Tenses 1

*Complete each sentence using either **yesterday** or **tomorrow**:*

1. Did you know I saw Steven _____?

2. What time will the lesson finish _____?

3. I was going to ring you _____, but I didn't have time.

4. Jean caught the bus to work _____ morning.

5. He would've liked to have seen you before you left _____, but never mind.

6. Both of us will be starting the new course _____ afternoon.

7. It will be almost impossible to finish this essay by _____!

8. I was in Bristol _____, visiting my old friends Raphael and Henry.

9. Are you sure you had an appointment booked for _____?

10. Jamie said that he should have finished mending the fence by _____ afternoon.

11. I couldn't ask you about the report _____ because you weren't in.

12. Samantha found out _____ that her parents are splitting up.

13. The concert starts at seven _____.

14. If I swim fifty lengths _____, my teacher said she will enter me into the competition.

15. I couldn't ring you _____ because I didn't have any credit on my phone.

Troubling Tenses – Mixed Tenses 2

*Complete each sentence using either **yesterday** or **tomorrow**:*

1. The Prime Minister gave a long speech about the economy _____. It was pretty boring!

2. When I saw you _____ I forgot to tell you that the conference won't be finishing until _____ night.

3. Sal should've told me _____ that she won't be able to pay us _____.

4. I could've had a lie in _____, if you weren't leaving so early.

5. Was it busy in town _____?

6. I'll be sorry to see you go when you leave _____.

7. If I can get a day off work _____, I'll be able to spend a bit of time with you.

8. If I could've bought you a birthday present _____ I would've done.

9. We're going on holiday to Venice _____.

10. I've never really liked Mexican food, but I really enjoyed the meal _____.

11. You must have rung the wrong number _____, because I was at home all morning.

12. Can you do the washing up that's been sitting here since _____, please?

13. We were gardening for about two hours _____ morning.

14. Could I have a go on your new computer game when I come round _____?

15. I think it should be quite sunny _____.

The Funny Noise –
Irregular Verbs in the Past Simple Tense

*a) Read the letter below from Alan to his friend Ethel. All the **irregular** verbs have the wrong ending – a **regular** '-ed' ending! Underline each one.*

b) Write the letter again, using the correct past simple form of each irregular verb.

Dear Ethel

I'm writing to tell you about something that happened yesterday. I getted up at the usual time – about 10am – haved a shower and maked breakfast. I eated a big bowl of cereal and some toast and watched TV for a while. Then I goed into the kitchen where I heared a funny noise. I thinked it comed from behind the cooker. I getted my tool box and moved the cooker out of the way.

The noise getted louder but I couldn't see anything. I ringed my uncle to ask his advice. He sayed that he thinked it could be a gas leak. When I heared this I just panicked! I putted the phone down, runned outside, getted in my car and drived to the local police station. I telled them about my gas leak but the constable losed his patience with me. He sayed that I should have phoned the gas company. He writed his report, then ringed the gas company for me.

Then I remembered that my house doesn't have gas – only electricity! I feeled really stupid and knowed that the constable would be angry with me for wasting his time, so I runned out of the police station while he ised still on the phone. I goed home to try to find out what the noise ised. On the way I buyed a newspaper and I readed about an escaped llama that breaked out of the city safari park last Wednesday.

When I getted home I putted my key in the door, turned it, goed inside and straight away heared that funny noise again. I holded my breath and opened the door slowly. Guess what? I finded the llama hiding in my cupboard! I letted him stay and he sleeped in my garden last night. The snoring ised so loud! This morning I taked him back to the safari park. They ared really pleased to see him again and gived me a reward of £50!

Hope you are well. Write soon and let me know how you are. Your friend,

Alan

Using Conjunctions – Mix & Match Cards 1

I don't like gardening,	**because** dirt gets in my nails.
Keesha wants a good job,	**because** she wants to earn a lot of money.
The bus was late,	**so** I was late for work.
I was worried about burglars,	**so** I fitted a burglar alarm.
The children are happy,	**because** it is Christmas Day tomorrow.
I used to go to London often,	**but** I don't any more.
I went outside,	**because** I needed some fresh air.
They gave me ten pounds	**and** a bottle of wine for my birthday.
The UK is a great place to live,	**because** the weather is so mild.
My cousin is getting divorced,	**but** she still loves her husband.
I don't watch TV very often,	**or** use the internet.
The dress was just right,	**so** I bought it.
You will have to work harder,	**or** you could lose your job.
I'm going to get a new car	**and** a CD player to put in it.
Her favourite song is 'Angels',	**because** it reminds her of her boyfriend.

Using Conjunctions – Mix & Match Cards 2

The car wouldn't start,	**so** I phoned the RAC.
I needed some advice,	**so** I asked my friend.
The CD was expensive,	**because** it was a new release.
It's really windy today,	**but** tomorrow should be a better day.
I went to bed at 10.30pm,	**because** I had to get up early the next day.
I don't like getting sunburnt,	**so** I always take my suntan lotion with me.
He didn't feel very well,	**so** he asked if he could leave the lesson.
They hardly ever come on time,	**but** I don't really mind.
Her project was interesting	**and** fun to look at.
The shop closes at 7.30pm,	**but** stays open late on Friday nights.
We don't know her,	**or** her family.
The concert finished early,	**so** we went for a meal.
I've got a hangover	**and** I don't feel well at all.
It's usually cold in here,	**because** he always leaves his windows open.
You might get in for free,	**or** you might have to pay.

Singular and Plural Nouns 1

a) Complete each sentence using either 'is' or 'are'.

b) Add 's' after the word 'pen' if it is a **plural noun**, but leave the space blank if it is a **singular noun**:

1. This _____ my pen _____.
2. There _____ two pen _____ on the table.
3. These pen _____ _____ on the table.
4. There _____ a few pen _____ on the table.
5. There _____ one pen _____ on the table.
6. There _____ lots of pen _____ on the table.
7. There _____ some big pen _____ on the table.
8. There _____ a pen _____ on the table.
9. There _____ a big pen _____ on the table.
10. This _____ his pen _____.
11. There _____ a box of pen _____ on the table.
12. That pen _____ _____ on the table.
13. Why _____ those pen _____ on the table?
14. These _____ the only pen _____ on the table.
15. There _____ a large quantity of pen _____ on the table.

Singular and Plural Nouns 2

a) Complete each sentence using either 'is' or 'are'.

b) Add 's' after the word 'pen' if it is a **plural noun**, but leave the space blank if it is a **singular noun**:

1. There _____ some pen _____ on the table.
2. There _____ not many pen _____ on the table.
3. This pen _____ _____ on the table.
4. There _____ not a single pen _____ on the table.
5. There _____ hardly any pen _____ on the table.
6. Those pen _____ _____ on the table.
7. This _____ their pen _____.
8. There _____ several pen _____ on the table.
9. There _____ twenty three pen _____ on the table.
10. This _____ the last pen _____.
11. This _____ the only pen _____.
12. There _____ a new pen _____ on the table.
13. There _____ a packet of pen _____ on the table.
14. There _____ another pen _____ on the table.
15. There _____ n't any pen _____ on the table.

Using Determiners 1

Read each of the following noun phrases. If they are not correct, write them again. Make sure that the noun agrees with the determiner:

1. a green bag　　　　　＿＿＿＿＿＿＿＿＿＿＿＿＿＿＿＿＿＿
2. some big table　　　＿＿＿＿＿＿＿＿＿＿＿＿＿＿＿＿＿＿
3. a beautiful pictures　＿＿＿＿＿＿＿＿＿＿＿＿＿＿＿＿＿＿
4. ten long dress　　　＿＿＿＿＿＿＿＿＿＿＿＿＿＿＿＿＿＿
5. the new black trousers　＿＿＿＿＿＿＿＿＿＿＿＿＿＿＿＿
6. an uncooked egg　　＿＿＿＿＿＿＿＿＿＿＿＿＿＿＿＿＿＿
7. a annoying person　＿＿＿＿＿＿＿＿＿＿＿＿＿＿＿＿＿＿
8. some nice people　　＿＿＿＿＿＿＿＿＿＿＿＿＿＿＿＿＿＿
9. some fresh sandwich　＿＿＿＿＿＿＿＿＿＿＿＿＿＿＿＿＿
10. a good programmes　＿＿＿＿＿＿＿＿＿＿＿＿＿＿＿＿＿
11. an interesting journeys　＿＿＿＿＿＿＿＿＿＿＿＿＿＿＿＿
12. a few young mans　　＿＿＿＿＿＿＿＿＿＿＿＿＿＿＿＿＿
13. lot of big problems　　＿＿＿＿＿＿＿＿＿＿＿＿＿＿＿＿
14. the left-hand side　　＿＿＿＿＿＿＿＿＿＿＿＿＿＿＿＿＿
15. a old suitcases　　　＿＿＿＿＿＿＿＿＿＿＿＿＿＿＿＿＿

Using Determiners 2

Read each of the following noun phrases. If they are not correct, write them again. Make sure that the noun agrees with the determiner:

1. a lot of noise _____
2. our two childs _____
3. some great offers _____
4. this tall buildings _____
5. the new magazines _____
6. a stupid mistakes _____
7. each pieces of paper _____
8. some fast car _____
9. all the right people _____
10. a new team leader _____
11. an complete mess _____
12. an early mornings _____
13. fewer problem _____
14. a hot cup of coffees _____
15. some terrible review _____

Using Determiners 3

Put a tick (✓) next to the phrase if it is correct and a cross (x) if it is not:

a	book	**his**	book
	books		books
	umbrella		umbrella
	umbrellas		umbrellas
	London		London
an	book	**this**	book
	books		books
	umbrella		umbrella
	umbrellas		umbrellas
	London		London
the	book	**which**	book?
	books		books?
	umbrella		umbrella?
	umbrellas		umbrellas?
	London		London?
some	book	**those**	book
	books		books
	umbrella		umbrella
	umbrellas		umbrellas
	London		London

Test Your Vocabulary Skills

The Joy of Abstract Nouns 1

Abstract nouns are nouns which don't have a physical form, for example, feelings (**happiness**), concepts (**democracy**) and qualities (**loyalty**).

Look at each adjective below and write a matching abstract noun:

adjective: *abstract noun:*

1. adventurous
2. amazing
3. able
4. angry
5. anxious
6. beautiful
7. brave
8. chaotic
9. compassionate
10. content
11. confident
12. courageous
13. curious
14. deceitful
15. democratic
16. determined
17. disappointed
18. educated
19. egotistical
20. energetic

The Joy of Abstract Nouns 2

Abstract nouns are nouns which don't have a physical form, for example, feelings (**happiness**), concepts (**democracy**) and qualities (**loyalty**).

Look at each adjective below and write a matching abstract noun:

adjective: **abstract noun:**

1. enthusiastic   _____
2. evil   _____
3. excited   _____
4. faithful   _____
5. fearful   _____
6. friendly   _____
7. generous   _____
8. good   _____
9. gracious   _____
10. happy   _____
11. homeless   _____
12. humorous   _____
13. imaginative   _____
14. inflated   _____
15. intelligent   _____
16. jealous   _____
17. joyful   _____
18. kind   _____
19. loyal   _____
20. lucky   _____

Emotions and Feelings 1

Match a sentence from section A with a sentence from section B:

Section A:

1. I'm happy because...
2. I'm sad because...
3. I'm afraid because...
4. I feel lonely because...
5. I'm disappointed because...
6. I'm worried because...
7. I'm confused because...
8. I feel hurt because...
9. I'm excited because...
10. I'm bored because...

Section B:

a) I have just lost £40.
b) I don't have anyone to talk to.
c) there's a spider in the bath.
d) I didn't get the job that I wanted.
e) the sun is shining.
f) I thought today was Wednesday.
g) my friends have been talking about me behind my back.
h) I haven't got any work to do.
i) we're all going on holiday tomorrow!
j) I don't know how I can pay my electricity bill.

Emotions and Feelings 2

Match a sentence from section A with a sentence from section B:

Section A:

1. I feel tired because...
2. I feel guilty because...
3. I'm surprised because...
4. I'm over the moon because...
5. I'm angry because...
6. I'm happy because...
7. I'm feeling down because...
8. I feel great because...
9. I'm shocked because...
10. I'm bored because...

Section B:

a) someone has stolen my new mobile phone.
b) I've been at work for twelve hours without a proper break.
c) I cheated during a test and got away with it.
d) I've just been to the gym and had a relaxing massage.
e) I have just won £2.5 million on the lottery!
f) my girlfriend has just dumped me.
g) I didn't realise I had two pounds in my pocket.
h) I'm home alone with nothing to do.
i) my dog has just had puppies.
j) I didn't know that we were related until last week!

Common Idioms 1

Idioms are spoken or written sentences where the meaning is not obvious from the individual words used.

Match the idioms with the meaning keywords below:

1. You've bitten off more than you can chew!
2. I've been burning the midnight oil lately.
3. He's feeling down in the dumps.
4. My brother's a couch potato.
5. It cost me an arm and a leg.
6. Can we let sleeping dogs lie?
7. That's a bit far-fetched.
8. Please stay in touch.
9. Shall we call it a day?
10. Don't count your chickens before they've all hatched.

Meaning Keywords:

a) Unbelievable.
b) Expensive.
c) Finish.
d) Working late.
e) Will be difficult.
f) Lazy.
g) Unhappy.
h) Write to me or call.
i) Forget the past.
j) Wait and see.

Common Idioms 2

Idioms are spoken or written sentences where the meaning is not obvious from the individual words used.

Match the idioms with the meaning keywords below:

1. Your account is in the red.
2. Fingers crossed!
3. It was a piece of cake!
4. Don't make a mountain out of a molehill.
5. Shut up!
6. The design was cutting edge.
7. Break a leg!
8. Take it easy, can't you?
9. It's been raining cats and dogs outside.
10. She's really tight-fisted.

Meaning Keywords:

a) Stop talking.
b) Easy.
c) Don't get angry.
d) Get some perspective.
e) Good luck for everyone.
f) Mean.
g) Modern.
h) Good luck for actors.
i) Heavy weather.
j) Overdrawn.

Understanding Quantities 1

Complete the sentences below using one of these words:

bottle   piece   cup   tub   ball   packet   pat   jar

book   plate   tube   can   half   bowl   dozen

1. A _____ of margarine.
2. A _____ of Coke.
3. A _____ of sweets.
4. A _____ of string.
5. A _____ of toothpaste.
6. A _____ of stamps.
7. A _____ of raspberry jam.
8. A _____ of lager.
9. A _____ of tea.
10. A _____ of bread and butter.
11. A _____ of soup.
12. A _____ eggs.
13. A _____ of material.
14. A _____ of butter.
15. A _____ of wine.

Understanding Quantities 2

Add an appropriate noun to each phrase:

1) A bar of _____
2) A cup of _____.
3) A glass of _____.
4) A loaf of _____.
5) A piece of _____.
6) A bottle of _____.
7) A pint of _____.
8) A litre of _____.
9) A bag of _____.
10) A packet of _____.
11) A ball of _____.
12) A jar of _____.
13) A lot of _____.
14) A plate of _____.
15) A slice of _____.
16) A dish of _____.
17) A pair of _____.
18) A group of _____.

19) A collection of _____.
20) A chunk of _____.
21) A bowl of _____.
22) A bouquet of _____.
23) A handful of _____.
24) A carton of _____.
25) A box of _____.
26) A can of _____.
27) A gallon of _____.
28) A pool of _____.
29) A barrel of _____.
30) A jug of _____.
31) A tank of _____.
32) A bundle of _____.
33) A pack of _____.
34) A drop of _____.
35) A pot of _____.
36) A tin of _____.

Shopping List – Mixed-up Quantities

Look at the shopping list. Write each phrase again using a more appropriate quantity word.

*For example: 'a tin of washing-up liquid' should be 'a **bottle** of washing-up liquid'.*

Shopping List:

1. a jar of crisps _____

2. a bottle of bread _____

3. a bag of chocolate _____

4. a packet of orange juice _____

5. a tin of ice cream _____

6. a can of chewing gum _____

7. a loaf of sandwiches _____

8. a packet of milk _____

9. a carton of jam _____

10. a bar of cake _____

11. a piece of lemonade _____

12. a bottle of cheese _____

13. a can of lettuce _____

14. a tub of fish _____

15. a box of baked beans _____

Family Matters (gap-fill) 1

Complete the sentences below using one of these words:

divorced   godson   boyfriend   godmother   single   ex-wife

cousin   sister-in-law   nephew   partner

Tim:

"My sister's son is my _____."

"My brother's wife is my _____."

"The woman I'm divorced from is my _____."

"The woman I live with now is my _____. We're not married or engaged though."

"My sister isn't in a relationship at the moment. She's _____."

Sally:

"The man I'm going out with is my _____."

"My aunt's daughter is my _____."

"The little boy whose christening I went to is my _____."

"My mum's old friend Paula is my _____."

"My mum and dad aren't married any more. They are _____."

Family Matters (gap-fill) 2

Complete the sentences below using one of these words:

engaged   widow   dysfunctional   ex-husband   fiancée   gay

great-grandfather   widower   girlfriend   children

Peter:

"My last partner was called Dave. He has two _____."

"I live with my current partner Brian. I'm _____."

"Brian's mum is dead. His dad Keith is a _____."

"My little sister and her boyfriend have just got _____."

"My grandma often talks about her dad. He was my _____."

Ellie:

"My mum has lived on her own for ten years since my dad died. She's a _____."

"I was married for six years. I don't really see Jon. He's my _____."

"My brother is always going on about Lena, his new _____."

"If I get engaged to my current partner Nick, I'd be his _____."

"Nick's family isn't really normal. You could say it's _____."

26.

My Relatives

Fill in the gaps below with the correct family word:

1. My grandma's granddaughter is my _____.
2. My son's grandmother is my _____.
3. My son's wife is my _____.
4. My mother's son is my _____.
5. My nephew's sister is my _____.
6. The man I'm married to is my _____.
7. My brother's wife is my _____.
8. The person I live with as if I'm married to them is my _____.
9. The man I used to be married to is my _____.
10. My grandfather's wife is my _____.
11. My mother's sister is my _____.
12. My father's father is my _____.
13. My cousin's father is my _____.
14. The boy I gave birth to is my _____.
15. My daughter's son is my _____.
16. The woman I married is my _____.
17. My son's sister is my _____.
18. My aunt's daughter is my _____.
19. My sister's husband is my _____.
20. My brother's father is my _____.

Word Pyramid – Parts of a Sentence

Complete the gaps to make a word pyramid:

1. A 2-letter preposition beginning with…

    i _____

2. A 3-letter common noun beginning with…

    j _____

3. A 4-letter adjective beginning with…

    r _____

4. A 5-letter proper noun beginning with…

    C _____

5. A 6-letter adverb beginning with…

    n _____

6. A 7-letter common noun beginning with…

    e _____

7. An 8-letter adverb beginning with…

    t _____

8. A 9-letter adjective beginning with…

    b _____

Adjectives and Synonyms 1

A **synonym** is a word or phrase that has either the same or a very similar meaning to another word or phrase. For example, 'nice' and 'pleasant'.

Look at the **adjectives** below and find a synonym for each one from this box:

> baffling   diverse   indefatigable   happy
> outgoing   green   genuine   prized
> unsatisfactory   loose   concealed   good-looking
> undercover   pleased   immature

1. disguised   _____
2. sociable   _____
3. authentic   _____
4. varied   _____
5. delighted   _____
6. hidden   _____
7. leafy   _____
8. childish   _____
9. cheerful   _____
10. valuable   _____
11. puzzling   _____
12. unacceptable   _____
13. baggy   _____
14. attractive   _____
15. tireless   _____

Adjectives and Synonyms 2

A **synonym** is a word or phrase that has either the same or a very similar meaning to another word or phrase. For example, 'nice' and 'pleasant'.

Look at the **adjectives** below and find a synonym for each one from this box:

> well-built   old   trustworthy   gifted
> uninteresting   terrible   authentic   modern
> scary   chilly   articulate   specialised
> pleasant   unworkable   unintentional

1. accidental
2. accomplished
3. technical
4. boring
5. fluent
6. lifelike
7. ancient
8. honest
9. nice
10. bad
11. frightening
12. contemporary
13. icy
14. strong
15. unrealistic

Advanced Homophones 1

Homophones are words that sound the same as each other, but have different spellings and meanings.

Write an English word that sounds the same as each of these words:

1. bow _____
2. birth _____
3. lays _____
4. faint _____
5. in _____
6. yolk _____
7. team _____
8. pie _____
9. chord _____
10. metre _____
11. I'll _____
12. fur _____
13. berry _____
14. draft _____
15. wet _____

Advanced Homophones 2

Homophones are words that sound the same as each other, but have different spellings and meanings.

Write an English word that sounds the same as each of these words:

1. gate   _____
2. heart   _____
3. desert _____
4. loo   _____
5. board   _____
6. flair   _____
7. whale   _____
8. sweet   _____
9. beat   _____
10. sore   _____
11. you'll _____
12. while _____
13. hire   _____
14. bite   _____
15. ale   _____

Onomatopoeia – List of Noisy Words

Onomatopoeic *words are words that sound like the noises they describe:*

baa	hiss	splat
bang	honk	splatter
bark	hoot	splosh
beep	howl	splutter
belch	hum	squawk
boing	ker-ching	squeak
boom	knock knock	squelch
brring	miaow	thud
bubble	mmm	thwack
burp	moan	tick tock
buzz	mumble	trickle
cackle	munch	twang
chirp	murmer	tweet
chomp	mutter	waffle
chortle	neigh	whimper
chuckle	oink	whirr
clang	parp	whizz
clap	ping	whoosh
clash	pitter patter	woof
clatter	plink plonk	yawn
click	plop	yelp
clip clop	pop	zip
clunk	purr	
cock a doodle doo	quack	
cough	ribbit	*My suggestions:*
crackle	rip	
creak	roar	_____
croak	rumble	
crunch	rustle	_____
ding dong	screech	
drip	shush	_____
fizz	slap	
fizzle	slither	_____
flutter	smack	
gasp	smash	_____
glug	snap	
groan	snarl	_____
growl	snore	
grunt	snort	_____
guffaw	snuffle	
gurgle	splash	_____

Onomatopoeia – Noisy Words

Match the noisy word on the left with a sentence on the right:

1. **beep**   a) I'm asking you politely to be quiet.
2. **chuckle**   b) It's not that boring, is it?
3. **clatter**   c) A cat having a nap with its owner.
4. **ding dong**   d) The sound of money being made.
5. **drip**   e) The march of time sounds like this.
6. **ker-ching**   f) Is that thunder in the distance?
7. **munch**   g) A guitar being played, but badly.
8. **purr**   h) An angry motorist or a wake-up call.
9. **rumble**   i) Can you answer the door, please?
10. **shush**   j) Dropping a dozen plates on the floor.
11. **snore**   k) Do up your coat – it's cold outside.
12. **tick tock**   l) When something is *quite* funny.
13. **twang**   m) The sound of a healthy appetite.
14. **yawn**   n) Sleeping like a baby.
15. **zip**   o) Turn off the tap properly after use to avoid this.

Talking about the Weather 1

Look at the following statements. What is the weather like in each situation?

For example: *"It's chucking it down."   It's raining.*

1. "It's a real pea-souper." _____
2. "What a lovely day." _____
3. "It's blowing a gale outside." _____
4. "I can only see a few metres in front of me." _____
5. "Wind's getting up." _____
6. "It's only spitting." _____
7. "It's all turned to slush." _____
8. "Whatever you do, don't stand under a tree." _____
9. "You might need an umbrella." _____
10. "Make sure you wrap up warm." _____
11. "Stay in the shade." _____
12. "It's really freezing outside." _____
13. "It's a scorcher." _____
14. "Looks like it might be a white Christmas after all." _____
15. "I'm boiling." _____

Talking about the Weather 2

Look at the following statements. What is the weather like in each situation?

For example: *"It's chucking it down."*   It's raining.

1. "It's a bit overcast."   _____
2. "It's quite chilly, isn't it?"   _____
3. "Let's go sledging."   _____
4. "It's really coming down now."   _____
5. "Look. It's hit that tree."   _____
6. "Nice weather for ducks."   _____
7. "Did you hear that? There must be a storm on its way."   _____
8. "You don't need a coat."   _____
9. "I'd better take a jumper, just in case."   _____
10. "It's definitely shorts weather."   _____
11. "Can you pass me the de-icer please?"   _____
12. "Turn up the air-conditioning, mum."   _____
13. "The sun's gone in now."   _____
14. "There are some people skating on the lake."   _____
15. "I think I'm going to melt."   _____

Test Your Spelling Skills

100 Commonly Misspelled Words

absence
accept
accidentally
acquit
address
already
amateur
analyse
apologise
apparent
apparently
appearance
appetite
appreciate
assassination
attached
attachment
believable
Caribbean
category
cemetery
changeable
chocolate
colonel
column
coming
deceive
decorate
definitely
development
disappear
discipline
discussion
dissatisfied

drunkenness
earring
eighth
embarrass
enough
government
grammar
guarantee
guerrilla
handkerchief
harass
height
heroes
humorous
hundred
hypocrisy
imagine
imitate
immediately
incidentally
independent
innocuous
inoculate
intelligence
lovely
millionaire
miniature
mischief
missile
moccasin
necessarily
niece
ninety
no one

noticeable
occasion
occurrence
omission
opposite
parallel
parliament
pastime
perceive
pigeon
pleasant
possessive
precede
principal (main)
rescind
restaurant
rhythm
sandal
satellite
similar
stationary (motionless)
stationery (pens, etc.)
stereo
succeeded
summary
supersede
surprise
temperature
whether
wholly
whose
wield

Be the Spell-checker 1 – Going on Holiday

Ever wanted to be a human spell-checker? Now's your chance!

Read the text below. There are twenty words spelt incorrectly. Underline each one and write the correct spelling above it:

I'm going on holday to France in Argust with my famly.

We are stayin on a new campsight for ten days.

My bruther and sister will be comming, but my cousin can't cos he is working.

We'll have to leeve erly to get the ferry – at about seven o'clok.

There will be over one hunded and forty carvans there.

I'm looking forard to goin in the swiming pool because I love divving.

It shud be a reelly good holeday.

Be the Spell-checker 2 – Shopping List

Ever wanted to be a human spell-checker? Now's your chance!

Read the text below. There are twenty words spelt incorrectly. Underline each one and write the correct spelling above it:

Shopping List:

Pasta sorce – tomatoe and mushrom

Ice creem – vanila and stawberry

Fruit – orangs, appuls, bananas, tangerines

Meat – steaks, sosages and burgers for the barbecue on Saterday

Brekfast cereals – corn flakes and musli

Crisps and choclate cake (for Jack's birthday on Firday)

Cofee, tea, suger, orange and pinapple squash, lemonade, and cola

Fresh vegtables – 2 bags of potatos, sweetcorn, carots, peas and salad

Be the Spell-checker 3 – Giving Directions

Ever wanted to be a human spell-checker? Now's your chance!

Read the text below. There are twenty words spelt incorrectly. Underline each one and write the correct spelling above it:

"How do you get to the bank from here...?"

"To get to the bank you nead to tirn left here then work for about 200 metes. Turn right onto Stockley Stret and you'l see the park on your left. Walk parst the main entrence to the park and turn rite into Bromley Avene. The bank is abbout 100 metre down Bromley Avenue. Its oppostite the post offise. It's not far from here – probaly about 15 minites if you walk quickley. Youd better hurry as I think it closes at five o'clok."

Be the Spell-checker 4 – School Days

Ever wanted to be a human spell-checker? Now's your chance!

Read the text below. There are twenty words spelt incorrectly. Underline each one and write the correct spelling above it:

"When did you leave school?"

"I left scool nearly fiteen years ago. My favuorite subjects was English, Franch and History. I enjoyed French becase it was intresting learning to speak a diferent langage and I had a good teecher. I didn't like Science or Maths because they were a bit harder and I didn like the teachers much. I'll newer forget when our clas went on a trip to Franse. We stayed in Paris for for nihgts. It was the fast time I'd been abroud. My fiends and I had so mach fun!"

A Letter to Aunt Monica

See if you can find all the spelling and punctuation mistakes in Sandy's letter:

25th september 2004

cardiff, uK

Dear aunt Monica

Thank you very much fo your letter. It was greet to get a letter from you. I am really enjoying University life. i have made some good fiends allready – expecially helen and marcus. Helen is form Manchester and Marcus comes from liverpool. His accent is reelly wierd.

yesterday we went to Cardiff to do som shoping. Everything is much more exspensive than back at home. – i miss Jamaica and of corse I miss You and my naughty little bruthers. Cardiff is a Big city – the capitul city of Wales. Wales is nex to Englund and a seperate country, but they are both part of the UK. It's confusing, isn,t it?

My course Is verry interesting.. i am leaning so much about the enviroment of this country. my Teachers are Good, accept I wish they would speek more slowly som of th time.,,   I can't always here everythng that they are saying. That's Why I'm using a small tape recorder to record every lecture8. Then I can listen to it in my Room as I stuidy. It's really helps.

Thank s for asking abot all my boyfrends !! No, – I haven,t met anone yet. I'm here to learn about the enviroment and practise my english, rathur than go out drinking in pubs and clubs with boys every night! I hope that i will fiind someone who shars my interests. Untill that time ; you will have to make do with me being a singl girl!

With Lots of Love to you and my Darling bruthers Roger an Paul, and all my family and frends there. I will see You very soon. Hope I will hear from you soon Too.'

Your loving Niece,

Sandy x x x x

Advanced Spelling Challenge 1

Look at the words below. There are five words spelt incorrectly in each box. Underline each one and write the correct spelling above it.

Note: this exercise does not include American English spellings.

---

fourth   chocolate   embarass   library   missile

comming   beleive   analise   deceive   curiculum

---

necesarily   leisure   genius   calender   imitate

ache   cooly   eightth   Febuary   colonel

---

manoevre   jewellery   disapear   fiveteen   guarantee

cinema   discipline   wierd   referal   vacuum

43.

Advanced Spelling Challenge 2

Look at the words below. There are five words spelt incorrectly in each box. Underline each one and write the correct spelling above it.

Note: this exercise does not include American English spellings.

---

receipt
receit   satellite   separate   women   pigeon
                                                    seperate   pidgeon

stereo   ninety   fulfil   mischief   favourite
                            fulfill   mischeif

---

magazine   exceed   belief   hundred   decorate
                            beleif   hunderd

grammar   Caribbean   wholly   year   attached
                Caribean   wholy   attatched

---

niece
neice   earring   fiery   rhythm   wiry
                                rythm

twelfth   quizzes   occurrence   similar   sergeant
twelth   ocurrence   sargeant

44.

Advanced Spelling Challenge 3

Look at the words below. There are five words spelt incorrectly in each box. Underline each one and write the correct spelling above it.

Note: this exercise does not include American English spellings.

broccoli	generaly	moccasin	appearance	enough
height	acheivement	exersise	comission	fourty

truly	rescind	seperation	quiet	purile
paralel	million	collectable	exagerate	liason

apetite	absence	disatisfied	necesary	wield
sandal	weather	quandry	though	suceeded

Advanced Spelling Challenge 4

Look at the words below. There are five words spelt incorrectly in each box. Underline each one and write the correct spelling above it.

Note: this exercise does not include American English spellings.

---

begining   millenium   liar   imediately   definitly

vegeteble   thought   publicity   lightning   liquefy

---

autumn   existence   inocuous   until   rasberry

preceed   conscience   acquit   beseige   adress

---

written   supercede   schedule   drunkeness   milionaire

incidentaly   category   cemetary   unique   profession

Seeing the Sights in London

Rearrange the anagrams below to find the names of twenty famous London sights:

1. HET DONLON YEE _____
2. HAKINGMBCU LACEPA _____
3. SHOESU FO LIMEANTPAR _____
4. GBI ENB _____
5. TS LAUP'S CHEDLATRA _____
6. NODOLN BGIDER _____
7. ROOLWATE BIRDEG _____
8. RODHASR _____
9. FOXDOR RETEST _____
10. ILDYLPAICC CUSCIR _____
11. AGAFLRTRA EUQARS _____
12. YEHD APRK _____
13. TS ESJAM'S KARP _____
14. ALNINOAT ARTEETH _____
15. NILATNAO TORRAPIT LEGALRY _____
16. VENTCO DARGEN _____
17. YALRO FALTESIV LALH _____
18. BOGLE REHETAT _____
19. LNOSEN'S MUNCOL _____
20. LEESITERC QEUSAR _____

Test Your Reading Skills

Any Answers 1

*Put a circle around the letter of the **best answer** to each question or comment below:*

1. Did you have a good flight?

a) It was cheap.
b) Terrible!
c) A good way to travel.
d) Yes, please.

2. Is this the way to the church?

a) It's near here.
b) He knows the way.
c) I often go here.
d) I don't think so.

3. I'm tired.

a) It's OK.
b) So was I.
c) It's boring.
d) Have a break.

4. Do you want to go out tonight?

a) Yes, really.
b) I'm not going.
c) No, really.
d) Not really.

5. How much sugar do you want in your coffee?

a) So much.
b) Not much.
c) Too much.
d) Little bit.

6. Where's the TV guide?

a) It doesn't know.
b) In the table.
c) On the table.
d) It's not usually there.

7. What time did your friends come round?

a) Later.
b) About eight o'clock.
c) Yesterday evening.
d) Two of my friends came.

8. Did you know that this restaurant is closing down?

a) Yes, I always knew.
b) No, I don't know.
c) What time?
d) No, I didn't know.

9. Do you want fries with that?

a) Thank you, my good man.
b) Yes, sir.
c) Thanks.
d) If you don't mind awfully.

10. There's someone outside.

a) Where are they?
b) Is there?
c) Is it?
d) He's outside.

Any Answers 2

*Put a circle around the letter of the **best answer** to each question or comment below:*

1. When are you getting married?

a) Not often enough.
b) Sometimes.
c) Sometime next summer.
d) Later on.

2. How's it going?

a) It went about an hour ago.
b) It's going with us.
c) The sun is shining.
d) Fine.

3. What's the weather doing?

a) It's chucking it down.
b) I'm boiling.
c) It's chucking it up.
d) It was raining yesterday.

4. Did you watch that DVD I lent you?

a) We didn't get started.
b) About half of it.
c) There was nothing to watch.
d) Yes, any time.

5. Can Anna stay for dinner?

a) Whatever she wants.
b) She's coming downstairs.
c) If she wants.
d) No, we're having dinner.

6. My brother has just bought a new house.

a) Really good.
b) Really?
c) What's his name?
d) That was great.

7. Everyone's gone out.

a) Oh. Do you know where?
b) Oh. They've taken their time.
c) It's early.
d) Why didn't they tell her?

8. Can you lend me a pound for the bus home?

a) In a few days.
b) Sorry, I can't come with you.
c) Here it is.
d) Here you are.

9. There's something wrong with my car.

a) I didn't know.
b) You should have known.
c) How do you know?
d) Did you know?

10. Did you leave the kitchen light on?

a) Yes, it was Paul.
b) Only by mistake.
c) The light was left on.
d) What a waste of money.

Any Answers 3

*Put a circle around the letter of the **best answer** to each question or comment below:*

1. The film starts in half an hour.

a) What time is it?
b) It's on time.
c) We'd better hurry then.
d) It's on soon.

2. Which bus goes to Liverpool?

a) The number 28 has gone.
b) I'm not sure.
c) We can't go by train.
d) The three o'clock is coming.

3. Have you ever been to Portugal?

a) Yes, an hour ago.
b) Two years ago.
c) Not really, no.
d) Only by road or rail.

4. I can't pay my gas bill this month.

a) Oh dear.
b) How nice for you.
c) That's odd.
d) Please pay it.

5. This is my brother, Simon.

a) How old are you?
b) Have you got any children?
c) Do you want to go out tonight?
d) Hi.

6. Do you want a lift to the concert?

a) Give me a lift.
b) I don't care.
c) No, I can't.
d) I'm alright, thanks.

7. Excuse me, where are the toilets?

a) Turn left and go through the double doors.
b) Turn left and go through a double doors.
c) Turn left and go through the double door.
d) Turn left and go through a double door.

8. Are you Natalie Brown?

a) No, he's upstairs in a meeting.
b) No, she's upstairs in a meeting.
c) No, they're upstairs in a meeting.
d) No, he's not here today.

9. See you tomorrow.

a) No way.
b) Really soon.
c) Why wait?
d) See you.

10. When does the next course start?

a) Two weeks ago.
b) Quite often.
c) As soon as possible, please.
d) The week after next.

Any Answers 4

*Put a circle around the letter of the **best answer** to each question or comment below:*

1. What do you want for dinner?

a) A potato and a cabbage.
b) Egg and chips.
c) A bowl of cereal.
d) A cup of tea.

2. When does this lesson finish?

a) It hasn't finished.
b) Tomorrow.
c) Quarter past.
d) It's two hours long.

3. Your brother has been caught speeding.

a) It's his own fault.
b) What time?
c) He should drive to work every day.
d) Why were you speeding?

4. I'd like two first class stamps, please.

a) What's your destination?
b) Two pounds, please.
c) That's fifty six pence, please.
d) I can't find any.

5. Can I take your order?

a) No, thank you.
b) Non-smoking, please.
c) No, we're next.
d) No, we haven't decided yet.

6. It's my birthday on Wednesday.

a) How old are you?
b) Well done.
c) How old were you?
d) You must be very old.

7. What time do you usually go to bed?

a) I'm not tired.
b) I get up at about half past six.
c) It varies.
d) I need at least eight hours sleep.

8. I need a new car.

a) Why not?
b) It's a good car.
c) Have you tried Sainsbury's?
d) I'll help him to find one.

9. Have you seen my keys?

a) It's in the kitchen next to the radio.
b) It's on the kitchen table.
c) They're in the kitchen with the radio.
d) They're on the kitchen table.

10. You're too late – the train's just gone!

a) Oh no!
b) Oh yes!
c) Where?
d) What time is it?

Any Answers 5

*Put a circle around the letter of the **best answer** to each question or comment below:*

1. How old are you?

a) One hundred and eighty.
b) I'm young.
c) Nearly eighteen.
d) I have eighteen years old.

2. My GP is retiring soon.

a) You'll have to find a new one.
b) He is very tired.
c) Do you know how often?
d) My doctor told me.

3. Chocolate cake is bad for you.

a) I can't eat it.
b) I'm too unhealthy.
c) I shouldn't eat chocolate.
d) No, it's not!

4. Did you book the holiday?

a) Yes, I have.
b) Yes, I did.
c) Yes, I'd like to.
d) Yes, I do.

5. Good morning, you're through to the council house. Which department, please?

a) I want the council house.
b) What's your name?
c) Good morning.
d) Housing, please.

6. I came to class early but there was nobody there.

a) Who was there?
b) Why were you early?
c) Why weren't they there?
d) Who was early?

7. What's your e-mail address?

a) www.purlandtraining.com.
b) 29 Spring Lane, Newcastle.
c) rach990@purlandtraining.com.
d) Yahoo and Hotmail.

8. Can I see your passport, Madam?

a) Why?
b) Here she is.
c) Why not?
d) Yes, of course.

9. I've broken my leg playing football.

a) You poor thing!
b) How's it going?
c) Why have you broken it?
d) Did you win?

10. Do you like rap music?

a) Yes, it's in the morning.
b) No, I haven't got it.
c) Quite often.
d) Some of it.

Reading Comprehension 1 – Bob Hunter's Family

Bob Hunter is forty years old. He lives in Derby with his wife and three children. His wife's name is Linda and she is an artist. Their eldest child, Richard, is studying Engineering at Derby University. Their middle child is called Claire. She's fourteen and a student at Derby Grammar School. Their youngest child is Sally, who is twelve. She enjoys horse-riding and cycling. Bob is an accountant and works for Toyota at Burnaston. He enjoys his job but always looks forward to the weekend, when he can spend some quality time on the golf course. He is a member of Mickleover Golf Club and has been playing since he was eleven years old.

Questions:

1. Who is the paragraph about?
2. How old is he?
3. Where does he live?
4. Is he married?
5. How many children does he have?
6. What is his wife's name?
7. What does his wife do for a living?
8. What is the name of their eldest child?
9. What subject is he studying?
10. How old is Claire?
11. Which school does she go to?
12. What is the name of their other child?
13. How old is she?
14. What hobbies does she enjoy?
15. What does Bob do for a living?
16. Which company does he work for?
17. Does he like working there?
18. What does he do at the weekend?
19. What is the name of his golf club?
20. At what age did he start playing?

Reading Comprehension 2 – The Car Thief

Samantha was walking home from work one day last month, when she saw a man who was trying to break into a car. She asked him what he was doing and he told her to, "Get lost!" She ran to a nearby shop and asked the owner to call the police, which he did immediately. When she went outside again she saw that both the thief and the car had gone. About ten minutes later, a police car stopped outside the shop. A policewoman got out and asked Samantha some questions about the incident. She asked her to give a description of the car and the thief. Samantha said that the car was a dark blue Ford Focus with the registration number TR03 RMN8. She said that it had a large scratch on the right hand side. She described the man as tall with short dark hair. She said that he was slim, looked about twenty-five years old and was wearing a blue denim jacket and black jeans. The policewoman wrote down everything in a notebook. Samantha felt a little shaken but was glad to be able to help. A few days later she found out that the thief had been caught in Newcastle and that the car had been returned to its owner, undamaged.

Questions:

1. Who is the paragraph about?
2. When did the incident happen?
3. Where was she going?
4. What was the man doing?
5. What did he tell her to do?
6. Who called the police?
7. When did the police arrive?
8. Did a policeman question Samantha?
9. What colour was the car?
10. What make of car was it?
11. On which side was the scratch?
12. What was the registration number?
13. Was the thief tall or short?
14. What was he wearing?
15. How did Samantha feel?
16. When was the thief caught?
17. Where was the thief caught?
18. What happened to the car?
19. Was the car damaged?
20. What was the thief's name?

Reading Comprehension 3 – A Lazy Holiday or an Exciting Holiday?

Anna:

"I'm planning my holiday for next summer and I don't know whether I should have a lazy holiday or an exciting one. Last year I went on holiday to southern Spain with my best friends, Joanna and Ling. We stayed in a brilliant four-star hotel, which had three swimming pools. It was quite expensive but we really enjoyed ourselves and we all got great suntans! This year, Joanna is going away with her parents to Greece so it'll be just Ling and me. Ling wants us to go on an adventure holiday in Africa, the type where you have to go walking in the desert and sleep out in the open. She said it would be interesting and better than having a lazy holiday because we would learn about the world around us and see some wild animals. I'm not sure whether I want to go to Africa. For me, a holiday means relaxing on a beach, not trekking across the middle of nowhere. Ling said that we'd see elephants and zebras and have some amazing experiences. I think she's bored of lying in the sun all day and fancies a change. I've got to make up my mind by next Monday at the latest so that she can book the tickets. It would cost £1,400 each to go to Africa, but less than half that amount for two weeks in Portugal."

Questions:

1. When is Anna going on holiday?
2. Name her two closest friends.
3. True or false – last year she went to northern Spain?
4. How many swimming pools did their hotel have?
5. Was the hotel expensive?
6. True or false – only Anna got a good suntan?
7. Where is Joanna going on holiday this year?
8. Who is she going with?
9. What type of holiday does Ling want this year?
10. Where does she want to go?
11. Does Anna want to go with her?
12. Why does Ling want to go on this type of holiday?
13. What does Anna enjoy doing on holiday?
14. What animals does Ling hope to see?
15. What sort of experiences does she expect to have?
16. When does Anna have to let Ling know about the holiday?
17. How much would it cost each of them to go to Africa?
18. Would it be cheaper to go to Africa or Portugal?
19. Do you think Anna should go to Africa with Ling? Why?/Why not?
20. Do you think Anna *will* go to Africa with Ling? Why?/Why not?

Reading Comprehension 4 – What Shall We Do Tomorrow?

Serena and George are on holiday in Devon, UK. Serena says to George:

Serena:

"I think tomorrow we can have a lie in until about 8.30, then have a shower, then have breakfast. If you don't mind, I'll have cereal and you can have a fry-up, but you'll have to cook it, as I can't stand cooking meat. After that, you can wash up, while I have a walk down to the village to get the papers. I'll get a Telegraph for me and a Mirror for you, as I know you like doing the crossword. When I get back I thought we could play tennis for a couple of hours. Then you can drive me to the coast, where we can find a nice restaurant to have lunch. I'll probably order a large salad and you can have a fresh seafood dish, if you like. After lunch I'll want to relax for a while and be alone, so you'll have to go out on your own somewhere. You should either explore the town, or go to the beach for a couple of hours. We'll meet up again at about 5 o'clock for dinner. Then I'll want you to take me out for a drink, or we could always go to the theatre. I think they've got a comedy on at the moment. After our evening out I'll be pretty tired so I'll probably just go straight to bed. I'm looking forward to a lovely day tomorrow, George, dear. Does everything sound alright to you?"

Questions:

1. Who is speaking?
2. Where are they having their holiday?
3. What time will they get up?
4. What does Serena want for breakfast?
5. What can George have for breakfast?
6. Who will make George's breakfast?
7. What will George do while Serena is getting the papers?
8. What paper will Serena get for herself?
9. Why will she get the Mirror for George?
10. How long will they play tennis for?
11. Where is Serena planning to have lunch?
12. What can George have for lunch?
13. What does Serena want to do after lunch?
14. What does she suggest that George can do?
15. What time will they meet up for dinner?
16. What does Serena want to do after dinner?
17. What type of play is on at the theatre?
18. What is Serena planning to do after that?
19. Do you think George will agree to all of Serena's plans? Why?/Why not?
20. Do you think they will both enjoy the day? Why?/Why not?

Reading Comprehension 5 – Looking for a Job

It's 7.30pm. Emma phones a recruitment agency and leaves the following message on their answerphone:

Emma:

"Hello. I wonder if you can help me. My name is Emma Heath. I'm looking for a job as an administrator. At the moment I'm working at a solicitor's as a clerk. Do you know Blame, Payne and Co.? I've been working there for about two years but there doesn't seem to be any chance of promotion, so I'm trying to find something else. The other thing is, I'm moving soon, so I'm looking for a job in Leicester. I would prefer it if it was in the city centre really. My current address is 23 Terraced Walk, Derby, DE23 3GP, but I'm going to be moving out on the 30th, and then I'll be living with my mum until I've found a house to rent in Leicester. After the 30th you'll be able to contact me at my mum's. Her address is 8 Cedars Lane, Swinscote, Derby, DE40 9UR. By the way, my mobile number is 079421 645784. If you do ring me on my mobile, please can you ring after six because I'll be at work all day and my boss doesn't know that I'm planning on leaving. My current salary is 11K per annum and I would like to find something for at least thirteen or more. I'll bring my CV in to your office once I've finished updating it. Oh yes, last month I went on a four-day intensive first aid course, which makes me fully qualified to give first aid."

Questions:

1. Who is the paragraph about?
2. Why does she leave the message?
3. What job does she do at the moment?
4. What job would she like to do?
5. Name the company that she works for.
6. How long has she been working there?
7. Why does she want to leave?
8. Which city is she moving to?
9. What is her address at the moment?
10. Is she planning to buy a house in Leicester?
11. What is her mum's address?
12. When can she be contacted there?
13. Add together the first four digits of her phone number.
14. When can she be contacted on her mobile number?
15. How much would she like her salary to increase by?
16. What is a CV?
17. What do the letters CV stand for?
18. Is Emma's boss upset that she will be leaving?
19. In your opinion, is Emma right to look for another job? Why?/Why not?
20. Do you think she will be happier living in Leicester? Why?/Why not?

Reading Comprehension 6 – How Much Money Do They Have?

Use only the following information to find the answers:

Tim has £3.47.

He gives £2 to **John**, who already had £10.75.

Tim's sister, **Clare**, takes £20 out of the bank and gives half to **Lisa**.

Lisa spends £4.99 on a t-shirt and gives the rest back to Clare, who then lends £2.50 to **Jalal**.

Jalal owes a pound to **his brother**, so he gives him three quarters of that.

John gives £5.58 to **Keith**, who needs it because he owes a fiver to **Kathy**.

She puts it with the 68p that she already has in her pocket, then withdraws £60 from a cashpoint and gives a quarter of that to **Laurie**, who spends a third and shares the rest equally between her cousins, Jalal and **Ruby**.

How much money does each person have now?

1. Tim has _____
2. John has _____
3. Clare has _____
4. Lisa has _____
5. Jalal has _____
6. Jalal's brother has _____
7. Keith has _____
8. Kathy has _____
9. Laurie has _____
10. Ruby has _____

Reading Comprehension 7 – When's Your Birthday?

Use the information below to find the date of each person's birthday:

Joe was born on the twenty-third day of the fifth month.

His wife **Colette**'s birthday is two days after that, which is five days before their wedding anniversary.

Conor's birthday is six days before Joe's.

Laura's birthday is three days before Christmas Day.

May's birthday is on the nineteenth day of the eighth month.

Sarah's birthday is exactly four weeks and one day later.

Leanne's birthday is on the day before Valentine's Day, while **her husband**'s birthday is four days after May's.

Tom's birthday is exactly a fortnight after Colette and Joe's anniversary, while **Mohammed** celebrates his birthday on the forty-second day of the year.

1. Joe's birthday is on _____.

2. Colette's birthday is on _____.

3. Conor's birthday is on _____.

4. Laura's birthday is on _____.

5. May's birthday is on _____.

6. Sarah's birthday is on _____.

7. Leanne's birthday is on _____.

8. Leanne's husband's birthday is on _____.

9. Tom's birthday is on _____.

10. Mohammed's birthday is on _____.

Reading Comprehension 8 – Checking Train Times

Sian phones her friend Khalid and leaves a message on his answerphone:

"Hi, Khalid. I've just checked the train times for Tuesday next week and I've found a train from Derby to Edinburgh that takes about four and a half hours. Well, four hours and twenty-three minutes to be precise. It leaves Derby at 9.16 in the morning and gets into Edinburgh at 13.39. You have to change once, at Newcastle. It gets into Newcastle at 11.52 and leaves at 12.01. The train to Newcastle is run by Virgin Trains and the train you get from Newcastle to Edinburgh is run by GNER. There is a faster service but it leaves Derby later in the morning – at 10.14 – and you have to change at Darlington. It gets into Darlington Station at 12.14 and then you've got a seven-minute wait before your next train leaves. It gets into Edinburgh at 14.21. If you get the first train I can meet you at two o'clock. My sister and her friend never finish work until half past two so they can only come with me to meet you if you get a later train. Let me know which train you're coming on. If you want to come later just let me know. I'll be in tonight until half eight-ish, then I'm going out with Michelle. Or you could give me a ring tomorrow night. I'll be at my mum's, on 0131 600 46220. I'm going there after work, so ring me any time after about quarter past six and you should catch me there. Oh yes, the number to find out train times is, er, 08457 484950. You could always give them a ring yourself and find out about a different time."

Questions:

1. Who is speaking?
2. Who does she leave a message for?
3. Where is her friend travelling from and going to?
4. How long exactly does the first journey from Derby to Edinburgh take?
5. How long exactly does the second journey from Derby to Edinburgh take?
6. How many changes are there during the first journey?
7. How long does it take the first train to get from Derby to Newcastle?
8. Where do you have to change during the second journey?
9. How long does it take the second train to get from Darlington to Edinburgh?
10. Which of the two trains taken during the first journey is run by Virgin Trains?
11. Write in words the time that the second train gets into Edinburgh.
12. What is the name of the other train company mentioned?
13. Do you know of a faster way to get from Derby to Edinburgh?
14. What time does the caller's sister finish work on Tuesdays?
15. If her friend gets the second train, how many people will meet him at the station?
16. What time is the caller going out tonight?
17. Who is she going out with?
18. When is the caller's friend hoping to travel?
19. When will the caller next be at her mum's?
20. What is the phone number you can call to find out train times?

Reading Comprehension 9 – First Day in Class

Carolina is telling Lizzie about the first lesson of her new English class:

"Well, I was nervous before it started. There were eight of us altogether, including the teacher. My teacher's name is Charlotte. She's only been working there for two months. She used to teach in Spain. The first thing we did was stand in a circle and we had to try to learn everybody's name, age and where they come from. I don't know if I can remember all of them, but I'll try. There was someone called Alexandre. He's from Portugal too and he's 23. No, he was 24. There was Mohammad, from Kirkuk in Iraq. He's 30 – two years older than me. There were two other women – Hélène and Yui-Gui. Hélène's 38 and comes from France. She was a bit loud and I didn't talk to her much. Yui-Gui was really nice. We worked together – she was my partner for some of the lesson. She's from China and used to live in Beijing before she moved to England. She's 41 years old and married with two children. Patrick came half an hour late. He's 57 and comes from Eritrea in Africa. Charlotte said that he's got to come on time if he wants to stay in the class. The other student was Kamal. He was very quiet and didn't want to tell anyone his age, but I asked him at break-time; he told me that he's 29. He's from Afghanistan."

Questions:

1. Where did Charlotte used to teach?
2. Which student was quiet and which was loud?
3. Which city and country does Mohammad come from?
4. Who is French?
5. Who is 28 years old?
6. What is the name of the teacher?
7. How old is Alexandre?
8. Who comes from China?
9. How many students were female and how many were male?
10. Where does Patrick come from?
11. In which city did Yui-Gui used to live?
12. Who is the oldest student in the class and who is the youngest?
13. How old is Hélène?
14. Who is Eritrean?
15. Who used to live in Spain?
16. Who is Portuguese?
17. How many children does Yui-Gui have?
18. Who is 29 years old?
19. Who came late to the class?
20. What is the average age of the students?

Reading Comprehension 10 – What's the Right Time?

Graham is telling his friend Marco about what happened yesterday:

"I woke up yesterday morning and looked at my alarm clock. It said 2.15pm! I couldn't believe it. I thought I was late for work, so I jumped out of bed and ran into the bathroom. The clock on the wall in there was two and a half hours ahead of the one in the bedroom. It was very confusing! I had a shower then went downstairs. The clock in the hall was an hour behind the one in the bathroom. When I went into the kitchen I looked at the clock on the microwave, which was three and a quarter hours ahead of the one in my bedroom. I found out later that day that my flatmate, Gordon, had changed all the clocks in my house for a joke. He thought it was very funny. In the living room the clock on the video said it was 3.30am, while in the guest bedroom the clock on the wall next to the window was two hours and twenty-five minutes slower than that. I went into the study and picked up my watch. It was eight hours ahead of the one in the kitchen. I was due at work at 8.30am and didn't want to be late. I went outside into the garden and looked in at the window of my shed. The clock on the wall in there was three hours behind my alarm clock. There was a postman walking past, but he didn't know the time. He said that when he left the sorting office an hour or two ago he thought it was about six o'clock. In the end I phoned my brother Alan in Toronto, Canada, and he was really annoyed because I'd woken him up, along with his whole family. He said it was 2.44 in the morning their time. I had forgotten that in Toronto they're five hours behind us. That's how I finally found out what time it was!"

What time was it... (use either 'am' or 'pm')

1. ...in the study?
2. ...in the living room?
3. ...in the guest bedroom?
4. ...in the hall?
5. ...in Toronto, Canada?
6. ...in the shed?
7. ...in the bedroom?
8. ...in the kitchen?
9. ...in the bathroom?
10. ...at the end of the story? (the right time!)

More questions...

11. What is Graham's friend called?
12. What time did Graham have to be at work?
13. Who changed the clocks in Graham's house?
14. Where does Graham's brother live?
15. Why was he angry with Graham?

Test Your Speaking & Listening Skills

A Fair Price?

A. Look at the shopping items below. In your opinion, what is a **fair price** for each one, and how much is the **maximum** that you would be willing to pay for each? Give feedback to the whole class.

                                                 Fair Price (£/p or $/c):   **Max. Price (£/p or $/c):**

A litre of milk –

A loaf of bread –

A kilo of beef –

A dozen (12) eggs –

A large bunch of flowers –

A newspaper –

6 apples –

A medium-sized box of chocolates –

12 bags of crisps –

A 2 litre bottle of diet cola –

A litre of petrol –

B. In groups of 4 or 5 learners, imagine that you are setting up a shop that will sell all of the above items (you could add some of your own to the list too). As a group, agree on a **fair price** for each one. Give feedback to the whole class.

C. Decide on some **special offers** that will persuade customers to come into your shop rather than going to a competitor's. For example, **BOGOF**, **3 for 2**, **Half Price**, and so on. How many special offers should you have and how long should they last for? How will they affect overall sales? Give feedback to the whole class.

D. In your group, visit a real shop or supermarket and compare their prices and offers with the ones you have agreed on. Do you need to rethink your plans in the light of this? Give feedback to the whole class.

Talking about a Picture or Object

Practise talking about a picture or object so that you can give a short two-minute talk all about it. Here are some questions to help you prepare:

What is it?

Whose is it?

What does it do?

How big is it?

What shape is it?

What colour is it?

How heavy is it?

How old is it?

Where did you get it from?

When did you get it?

Why did you get it?

How did you get it?

How much did it cost?

How much is it worth now?

Why did you choose to talk about it?

What does it mean to you?

Tell a short story about it – give an example of when it was useful to you.

Summary:

What is it? (PURPOSE)

Describe it (DESCRIPTION)

Why is it important? (USES)

Tell a story about it (DEMONSTRATION)

Test Your Research Skills

Quick Quiz 1

Have fun with this quick quiz. It's ideal for team or individual use:

1. What is the capital city of the UK?
2. What colour is grass?
3. Write five different prepositions.
4. Write five different things that you can find at the dentist's.
5. What can you do at a train station?
6. Write five different things beginning with the letter 'a'.
7. Write the names of three different rivers in England.
8. What is the first day of the week?
9. John was born in May 1926 and died in October 2001. How old was he when he died?
10. Name an animal that goes 'neigh'.
11. In which room of your house can you watch TV?
12. Add together £2.40 and £4.60.
13. Is '23' an odd or an even number?
14. Write this time in words: 8.45 pm.
15. Write this number in words: 1,234.
16. What is John Major famous for?
17. How many vowels are there? Name them all.
18. Spell the word 'accommodation'.
19. What is the opposite of 'big'?
20. Who is the tallest person in your team?

Quick Quiz 2

Have fun with this quick quiz. It's ideal for team or individual use:

1. What is the capital city of France?
2. What colour is the sky at the moment?
3. Write five different sports.
4. Write five different things that you can find in a kitchen.
5. What can you do at a petrol station?
6. Write five different things beginning with the letter 'o'.
7. Which river flows through London?
8. What is the tenth month of the year?
9. Bob was born in March 1943 and died in January 1987. How old was he when he died?
10. Name an animal with stripes.
11. In which room of your house do you go to sleep?
12. Add together £5.67 and £14.48.
13. Is '98' an odd or an even number?
14. Write this time in words: 3.18 am.
15. Write this number in words: 192.
16. Who is the Chancellor of the Exchequer in the UK?
17. How many hours are there in one week?
18. Spell the word 'proposition'.
19. What is the opposite of 'far'?
20. Who is the oldest person in your team?

Quick Quiz Template

Try making your own quick quiz (for team or individual use) with this handy template:

1. What is the capital city of...? (e.g France)

2. What colour is...? (e.g. milk)

3. Write five different... (e.g. nouns, adjectives, adverbs, prepositions)

4. Write five different things that you can find... (e.g. at a cinema)

5. What can you do at...? (e.g. a museum)

6. Write five different things beginning with the letter... (e.g. 'r')

7. A geography question (e.g. 'Name a river in Africa')

8. A question using ordinal numbers (e.g. 'What is the fourth letter of the alphabet/day of the week/month of the year?' etc.)

9. How many years has 'x' been married...? Or how old is 'x'...?
(Make up a person and their date of birth or the date when they got married and ask how long ago it was from today's date)

10. A question about the animal kingdom, or about transport (e.g. 'Name an animal that lives underground' or 'How many wheels does a car have?')

11. In which room of your house can you...? (e.g. have a bath)

12. Numbers – add together 'x', 'y' and 'z'... (or subtract, multiply, divide, etc.)

13. Numbers – is 'x' an odd or an even number? (e.g. '5' is an odd number and '6' is an even number)

14. Write this time in words... (e.g. '4.15pm' in words is 'four fifteen pm' or 'quarter past four pm')

15. Write this number in words... (e.g. '2,310' in words is 'two thousand, three hundred and ten')

16. A general knowledge, history or arts question (e.g. 'What did Van Gogh do for a living?')

17. How many...? (e.g. 'How many people are there in this room?')

18. Spell the word... (e.g. 'entertainment')

19. What is the opposite of...? (e.g. the opposite of 'hot' is 'cold')

20. Who is the... person in your team? (e.g. oldest, richest, nicest, etc.)

Alphabet Quiz 1

All the answers begin with successive letters of the alphabet in this fun team quiz:

A	A place where a plane comes in to land.
B	This appears if you cut yourself.
C	A vegetable that is orange in colour.
D	A white bird that is a symbol of peace.
E	London is the capital city of this country.
F	A person that you can talk to, spend time with, and share things with.
G	The opposite of 'stop'.
H	You wear this on your head!
I	A country near to the UK. Its capital city is Dublin.
J	The first month of the year.
K	Something that children go and fly in the park.
L	A large vehicle used for transporting goods.
M	You spend this at the shops.
N	The opposite of 'always'.
O	A fruit and a colour.
P	Something that you can hang on your wall at home.
Q	What I'm asking you now!
R	A flower that has sharp thorns.
S	A place in the garden where you can keep tools and a lawnmower.
T	A type of shoe that is worn for running or playing sports.
U	This is how you feel when you are sad or start crying.
V	You sprinkle this on fish and chips along with salt.
W	A drink that is made from grapes. Can be red or white.
X	A musical instrument made up of metal or wooden bars.
Y	Bananas are this colour.
Z	Something you find on a pair of trousers.

Alphabet Quiz 2

All the answers begin with successive letters of the alphabet in this fun team quiz:

A	A foreigner, or someone who comes from another planet.
B	A place where you can deposit money.
C	A family pet who might chase birds and mice.
D	A large port in the south-east of the UK.
E	A popular soap opera broadcast on BBC1.
F	The last day of the working week.
G	The opposite of 'rough'.
H	You need this to pump blood around your body.
I	A European country. Its capital city is Rome.
J	Trousers; usually made of denim.
K	You use this to boil water in the kitchen to make a cup of tea.
L	This is what you get when you borrow money from the bank.
M	Pork, beef, chicken and ham are all types of this.
N	Preposition. The opposite of 'far'.
O	The first number.
P	Something that you open at Christmas or on your birthday.
Q	You stand in this when you wait in line at a supermarket.
R	A colour that symbolises the Communist party.
S	The name of woolly animals who love to eat grass.
T	Mr, Mrs, Ms, Dr, and Rev are all examples of this.
U	How to describe someone who is not attractive.
V	A city in Italy that is famous for its canals.
W	A season. In England it is cold and frosty.
X	You have this if you have a special quality that is indescribable.
Y	Something you say to agree with people.
Z	A black and white animal.

Alphabet Quiz 3

All the answers begin with successive letters of the alphabet in this fun team quiz:

A	A continent where you might see some penguins.
B	You can hear these being rung before a church service.
C	A fortress which kept out invaders in times gone by.
D	The animal commonly known as 'man's best friend'.
E	You need these to hear anything!
F	Something that you don't have to pay for can be described as this.
G	A relaxing game played over eighteen holes.
H	Where you end up if you break your leg and need an operation.
I	The name for someone who is really foolish.
J	You tell this to make somebody laugh.
K	A place where a dog may sleep.
L	There are many different ones spoken throughout the world.
M	A famous board game in which you have to buy properties and build hotels.
N	A bird will build this out of twigs for its family to live in.
O	A meal made from eggs and milk. You can add cheese, tomatoes, ham, etc.
P	You usually have two of these at the top of your trousers and one at the back.
Q	A major city in Canada.
R	Used to draw straight lines, or a King or Queen.
S	The opposite of 'weak'.
T	You produce these when you cry.
U	A very useful thing to have if it starts raining!
V	A type of material that feels very soft to the touch.
W	Rain, sunshine, thunder, cloud cover, and drizzle are all types of this.
X	This is a kind of photograph showing the inside of your body.
Y	There are twelve months in every one.
Z	The number before 'one'.

Wordsearch Fun

Title: _____

1. _____
2. _____
3. _____
4. _____
5. _____
6. _____
7. _____
8. _____
9. _____
10. _____

11. _____
12. _____
13. _____
14. _____
15. _____
16. _____
17. _____
18. _____
19. _____
20. _____

Design a Board Game

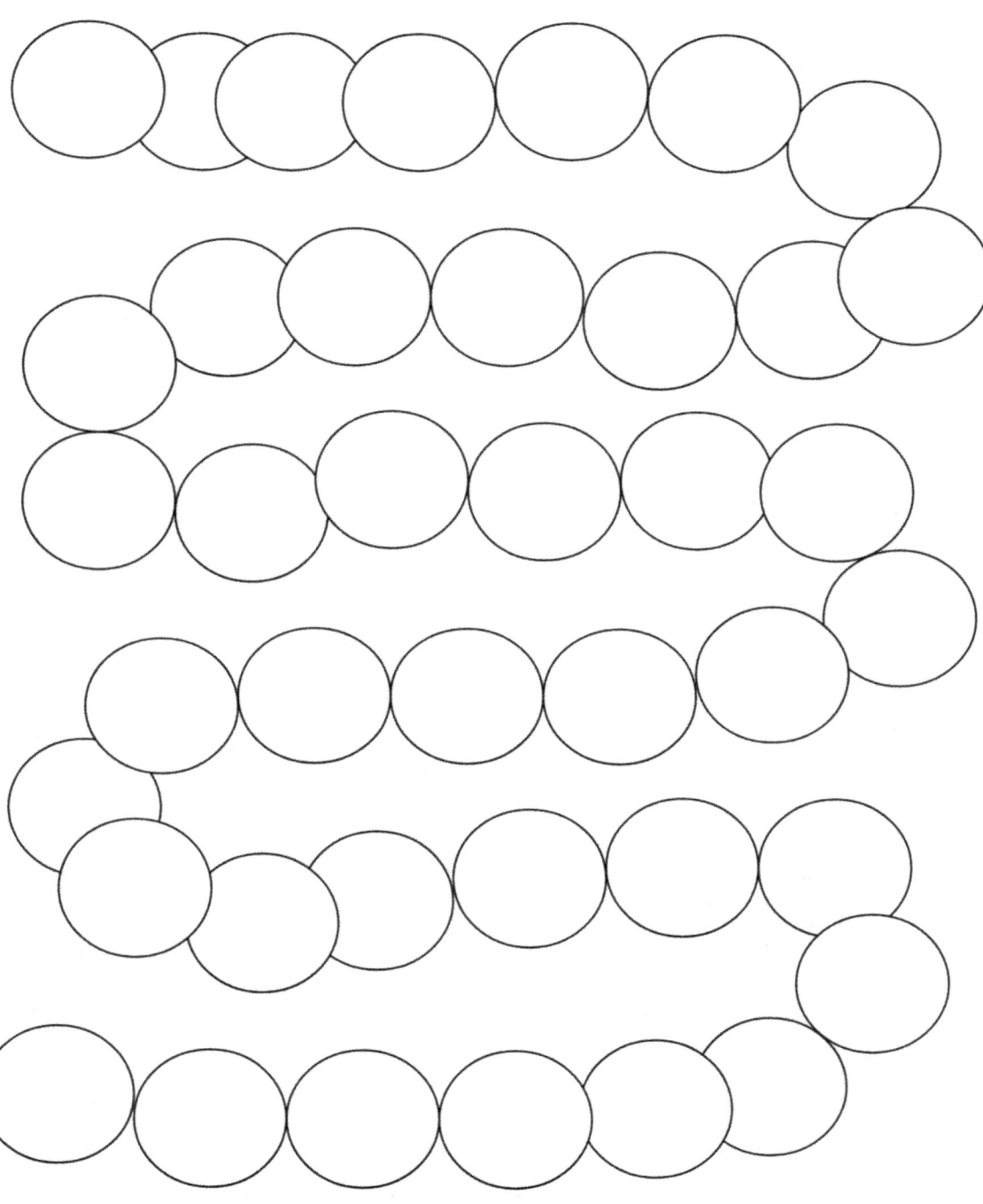

Interesting Place Names 1

Below is a list of towns and villages in England, Scotland and Wales.

However, among the real place names there are up to ten fake names. Using an atlas of Great Britain, find any fake names and put a tick next to them:

- ☐ Ache
- ☐ Bride
- ☐ Bottoms
- ☐ Yellow Ochre
- ☐ Evenjobb
- ☐ Macduff
- ☐ Idle
- ☐ St Bees
- ☐ Providence-under-Lyme
- ☐ Widow's Elbow

- ☐ Yelling
- ☐ Very i' th' Marsh
- ☐ Bluebells
- ☐ Upper Friendship
- ☐ Never Haddon
- ☐ Bell o' th' Hill
- ☐ Throp
- ☐ Wobbling Abbingdon
- ☐ Red Ball
- ☐ Anna Valley

Interesting Place Names 2

Below is a list of towns and villages in England, Scotland and Wales.

However, among the real place names there are up to ten fake names. Using an atlas of Great Britain, find any fake names and put a tick next to them:

- ☐ Kelly
- ☐ London Apprentice
- ☐ Beer
- ☐ Stanley Crook
- ☐ Belchford
- ☐ Much Hoole
- ☐ Norton-Juxta-Twycross
- ☐ Bishop's Itchington
- ☐ Clopton Corner
- ☐ Read
- ☐ Watermillock
- ☐ Little Wilbraham
- ☐ Weston-under-Lizard
- ☐ Trumpet
- ☐ Inkpen
- ☐ River
- ☐ Pratt's Bottom
- ☐ Homer
- ☐ Rose
- ☐ Shilbottle

Classic Books 1

Match the classic book with its author:

1. Daniel Deronda
2. Alice's Adventures In Wonderland
3. The Brothers Karamazov
4. Frankenstein
5. War and Peace
6. Our Mutual Friend
7. The Portrait of a Lady
8. Ivanhoe
9. The Wind in the Willows
10. Wuthering Heights
11. Sense and Sensibility
12. Winnie-the-Pooh
13. Treasure Island
14. Tess of the D'Urbervilles
15. Ulysses

a) Mary Shelley
b) Charles Dickens
c) George Eliot
d) Jane Austen
e) Kenneth Grahame
f) Fyodor Dostoyevsky
g) Emily Brontë
h) Leo Tolstoy
i) Lewis Carroll
j) Thomas Hardy
k) Henry James
l) James Joyce
m) Walter Scott
n) A A Milne
o) Robert Louis Stevenson

Classic Books 2

Match the classic book with its author:

1. The Secret Garden
2. Rebecca
3. 1984
4. Of Mice and Men
5. The Pilgrim's Progress
6. Lord of the Flies
7. As You Like It
8. The Lord of the Rings
9. Brave New World
10. Little Women
11. Kidnapped
12. David Copperfield
13. Crime and Punishment
14. The Mill on the Floss
15. Anna Karenina

a) Charles Dickens
b) George Orwell
c) George Eliot
d) William Golding
e) Daphne Du Maurier
f) John Steinbeck
g) Frances Hodgson Burnett
h) John Bunyan
i) Fyodor Dostoyevsky
j) Aldous Huxley
k) William Shakespeare
l) Leo Tolstoy
m) J R R Tolkien
n) Louisa May Alcott
o) Robert Louis Stevenson

The Life of Charles Dickens

Use a library facility or the internet to find the answers to these questions:

1. Where was Charles Dickens born?
2. When was he born?
3. What were his parents called?
4. Name two schools that he attended.
5. Where did the twelve-year-old Dickens work?
6. Name two other jobs that he had.
7. As a young writer, what was Dickens's pseudonym?
8. What was the name of Dickens's first love?
9. Which character did she inspire and in which novel?
10. What was his wife's name?
11. In what year were they married?
12. Name three of Dickens's ten children.
13. Name three novels by Charles Dickens.
14. In which novel do we meet the unscrupulous Sir Mulberry Hawk?
15. Which miserable Dickens character snarls: "Every idiot who goes about with 'Merry Christmas' on his lips, should be boiled with his own pudding, and buried with a stake of holly through his heart."? In which novel does he appear?
16. In what year did Dickens's father die?
17. Name the house on Gravesend Road in Kent that Dickens coveted as a child and bought in 1856.
18. In what year did Dickens separate from his wife Catherine?
19. Name the actress with whom Dickens spent the rest of his life.
20. When and where did Dickens die?

An A-Z of English Slang Terms – Part 1

Write a definition for each of the following slang terms.

Note: (n.) means the word is a noun and (a.) means it is an adjective:

A	argy bargy (n.)	_____
B	belly button (n.)	_____
C	clanger (n.)	_____
D	dog's breakfast (n.)	_____
E	easy peasy (a.)	_____
F	five finger discount (n.)	_____
G	gee gee (n.)	_____
H	humungous (a.)	_____
I	icky (a.)	_____
J	joanna (n.)	_____
K	knuckle sandwich (n.)	_____
L	lounge lizard (n.)	_____
M	monkey suit (n.)	_____

Extra time: write three sentences using each slang term.

An A-Z of English Slang Terms – Part 2

Write a definition for each of the following slang terms.

Note: (n.) means the word is a noun, (a.) means it is an adjective and (v.) means it is a verb:

N	nifty (a.)	_____
O	oomph (n.)	_____
P	pug ugly (a.)	_____
Q	quack (n.)	_____
R	rust-bucket (n.)	_____
S	spare tyre (n.)	_____
T	toodle-oo! (interjection)	_____
U	upchuck (v.)	_____
V	vamoose (v.)	_____
W	whatchamacallit (n.)	_____
X	Xmas (n.)	_____
Y	yuppie (n.)	_____
Z	zillionaire (n.)	_____

Extra time: write three sentences using each slang term.

Australian English Slang Terms – Part 1

Match the Australian slang term on the left with the correct meaning on the right:

1. footy
2. a barbie
3. fair dinkum
4. an earbashing
5. Aussie
6. a cobber
7. heaps
8. moolah
9. a dipstick
10. a dunny
11. the Outback
12. a Pom
13. a mongrel
14. to veg out
15. Down Under

a) a barbecue
b) an idiot
c) to rest and relax, especially watching TV
d) a lot
e) a friend
f) money
g) Australian
h) an English person
i) Australian Rules Football
j) true; genuine
k) a sustained period of nagging
l) a horrible person
m) an outside toilet
n) Australia and New Zealand
o) the interior of the continent of Australia

Australian English Slang Terms – Part 2

Match the Australian slang term on the left with the correct meaning on the right:

1. a chook   a) a pub
2. a rellie   b) Australia
3. "G'day"   c) a fight
4. grog   d) a person with bad manners
5. a roo   e) an informal greeting
6. a joey   f) to become angry
7. a blue   g) beer or alcoholic drink
8. "No worries"   h) a strong term of agreement
9. Oz   i) a postman
10. a boozer   j) a chicken
11. to spit the dummy   k) the name for a baby kangaroo
12. a yobbo   l) a member of your family
13. a postie   m) a university
14. "Too right!"   n) a kangaroo
15. a uni   o) a friendly term meaning "No problem"

Famous Quotations

Match these famous quotations with the person who said them:

1. 'England and America are two countries separated by a common language.'
2. 'Consistency is the last refuge of the unimaginative.'
3. 'Courage is the art of being the only one who knows you're scared to death.'
4. 'The great thing about a computer notebook is that no matter how much you stuff into it, it doesn't get bigger or heavier.'
5. 'Men are not prisoners of fate, but only prisoners of their own minds.'
6. 'Eighty percent of success is showing up.'
7. 'Imagination is more important than knowledge.'
8. 'Freedom is not worth having if it does not include the freedom to make mistakes.'
9. 'If I were two-faced would I be wearing this one?'
10. 'History will be kind to me for I intend to write it.'
11. 'When you are right you cannot be too radical; when you are wrong, you cannot be too conservative.'
12. 'If we observe, we shall find that all human virtues increase and strengthen themselves by the practice of them.'

A – Winston Churchill   B – Socrates   C – Harold Wilson

D – Franklin D Roosevelt   E – Bill Gates   F – Mahatma Gandhi

G – George Bernard Shaw   H – Oscar Wilde   I – Albert Einstein

J – Martin Luther King Jr.   K – Woody Allen   L – Abraham Lincoln

Holidays and Special Days in the UK

Below is a list of holidays and special days that are celebrated in the UK each year. Work with a partner to find the correct dates and find out what is special about each day:

Holiday or Special Day:	Date:
New Year's Day	
St Valentine's Day	
St David's Day	
Pancake Day (Shrove Tuesday)	
St Patrick's Day	
Mother's Day	
British Summer Time Starts	
Good Friday	
Easter Sunday	
Easter Monday Bank Holiday	
St George's Day	
May Day Bank Holiday	
Spring Bank Holiday	
Father's Day	
Longest Day (Summer Solstice)	
August Bank Holiday	
British Summer Time Ends	
Hallowe'en	
Bonfire Night	
Remembrance Sunday	
Shortest Day (Winter Solstice)	
Christmas Eve	
Christmas Day	
Boxing Day	
New Year's Eve	
My birthday	
My friend's birthday	
My teacher's birthday	

bingo!

Choose 15 numbers between 1-90 and write them in the boxes below:

---✂---

bingo!

Choose 15 numbers between 1-90 and write them in the boxes below:

---✂---

bingo!

Choose 15 numbers between 1-90 and write them in the boxes below:

Games for the Classroom

Speaking & Listening Skills

I-Spy

Students can lead this very simple game where they think of something that they can see in the classroom (or wherever you are) and the others have to guess what it is. Students give a clue by saying the first letter, for example, if they are thinking about the clock on the wall, they would say, 'I spy with my little eye, something beginning with C.' A quick game that gets the students thinking about the vocab relating to their immediate environment.

Class Secrets

Get the group together and ask for a volunteer to leave the room. Once they've gone, think of a 'secret' about that person, for example it's their birthday, or they're having an affair with the college principal. That kind of thing. When they come back in, they have to guess the secret truth about themselves by asking questions. The rest of the group give clues. A great ice-breaker, this one always raises a laugh.

Simon Says

A party game that works well with English students as a way of practising listening to and understanding commands. The teacher says a number of simple commands, such as, 'Put your hands on your head', 'Stand on one leg' or 'Start humming', and the students have to do what you say – but only if you have prefaced the command with 'Simon says...'. If you don't say 'Simon says...' and the student follows the command, they are out, and the game resumes until there is a winner.

Party Invitations

The whole class sits in a circle. Tell them that it's your birthday next week and that you're planning a birthday party. They are all invited... but on one condition. They must bring you a present, and it must be something that you really want. Each student in turn tells you what they will bring to give you on your birthday. You will either tell them that they can come, or that they are not invited. This depends on what they offer to bring you. The item they're going to bring must begin with the same letter as your first name. If it does, they can come; if it doesn't, they can't. For example, if your name is Lucy and they offer to bring 'a lemon' as a present, they will be welcome. If they offer to bring 'a bottle of wine' they will be given short shrift! This game is hilarious, as some students will twig onto your 'unspoken rule' fairly early on, while some won't get it at all, however obvious you make it!

Something's Different

Get the whole class together. Ask one of them to leave the room, then get the remaining students to change five things about the classroom. For example, you could put a chair on a table, or get two students to swap jumpers, or anything – so long as it's not too subtle. Then bring the student back in and get them to guess what changes you have made.

Whispering Trees

Get the students standing in a line. Stand at one end and whisper a short phrase or sentence

Games for the Classroom

in the ear of the student next to you. For example, you could say, 'My dad once met Bernard Cribbins in a bus queue in Dover.' Each student repeats the phrase to their neighbour until you get to the end of the line, when the last student tells the class the sentence they heard, and you can reveal what the original sentence was. A good game for practising listening and speaking skills.

What's Going On...?

Probably better for an intermediate or advanced class, this one. Prepare twenty questions, based on what is happening in the news (be it local, national or world news). You could include spelling questions too, and questions about different members of the class, for example, 'Which country does Louisa come from?' Split the class into two teams and you're ready to play. Give five points for a correct answer, and bonus points at your discretion for any extra information that the students give in their answers. If the first team doesn't know the answer, hand it over to the other team for a bonus point.

My Butler Went To Meadowhall

The title refers to Meadowhall shopping centre near Sheffield. The game is really just a version of My Grandmother Went To Market. Students sit in a circle, away from desks and paper, and so on. Tell the students that you teach because you love it and don't need the money as you are actually rather well off. In fact, you have a butler who goes up to Meadowhall every Friday to go shopping for you, and he buys you lots of different things. This week, however, you can't decide what to buy, so you are asking the students to help you. You are going to make a list. Start with saying, 'My butler is going to Meadowhall on Friday and will buy me... (think of any item that you can buy in a shop).' The next person has to say, 'Your butler is going to Meadowhall on Friday and will buy you...' whatever you said, plus an item of their own. The list goes around the circle until the last person has to remember the whole list of items. Students usually give prompts if their fellow students are struggling. A good vocabulary game, as well as being fun and a test of the memory. Plus they get a laugh thinking about your (imaginary – unless you really have one...?) butler.

What's In The Bag...?

Have a 'lucky dip' style bag, or box, which you can use from time to time for this quick activity that draws the class together in mutual curiosity. Put something different in the bag (or box) each time, for example, a paper clip, or an orange. Students take it in turns to feel inside the bag (or box) – without looking – and then describe what the object feels like and what they think it is. This activity can easily be handed over to the students for them to facilitate among themselves, even using items that they have brought in from home.

The Yes/No Game

An old favourite from TV, this is great for practising question and answer forms. Get students up to the front of the class one at a time and ask them questions, about themselves, the weather, the school or college – anything. The student must reply verbally but cannot say the words 'Yes' or 'No'. If they do, they are out. Ask someone to act as the timer (and as the 'gong' or 'buzzer' when each player slips up and is out), and write the times for how long each student managed to go without saying 'Yes' or 'No' on the board. If the students get the hang of this game they could play it in pairs, with one asking the questions and the other answering, before swapping over roles.

Games for the Classroom

Audio Pictures

Get the students into pairs, then give one half of the pair a picture from a magazine, for example, a man wearing a hat and coat and playing the piano. They have to describe what they can see, in detail, without showing the picture to their partner, who draws a sketch based on the description. At the end of the description they compare their pictures, before swapping roles. At the end of the session the whole class can see how close all the drawings were to their originals. A good activity for practising communication and listening skills, and giving descriptions.

Our Living Photo Album

Ask each student to bring in one or more photographs of something that is important to them, that you can keep to put into a class photo album. Give them time to prepare a two-minute talk about their photograph, which could be, for example, of a place, or a family member or an event that has touched their life. Then sit in a circle with all the students and your 'living photo album' will come to life, as each student in turn explains why their photo is important or memorable to them. You could make a display with the pictures, or literally fill an album with them that everyone can enjoy looking at. Explain that you will give the photos back at the end of the course (or even at the end of the week). This is a good activity to help a relatively new group get to know each other.

Reading and Writing Skills

Ace Anagrams

Students at all levels enjoy puzzling over this game. It's also a good way to get them looking in their dictionaries. Your students suggest nine letters at random, either vowel or consonant, which you write on the board. (Or you could have cards with them on if you're really organised!) In small groups the students have five minutes to come up with as many (real) words as they can from the original nine letters. The team with the most words spelt correctly gets a point, and the next round begins.

Hangman

Another good letters-based game. It's good because students can get up and lead this one just as well as the teacher. It's also good because it's quick and can pull students together for a quick bit of group work just before going home. Think of a word or phrase and draw a number of dashes on the board that corresponds to the number of letters. The other students suggest one letter at a time. If they are correct you have to fill in the letter on the board in its correct place. If they are incorrect you draw part of the hangman shape. Students can take a guess if they know the word. The person who guesses correctly steps up to the board to think of a word for the next session.

What Time Is It On...?

A good one for testing telling the time, and as a general reading comprehension using realia. Select a page from the Radio Times, or any English language TV guide and photocopy it so that each student can have a copy. Split the group into two teams and ask them questions based on the programme information given in the TV guide. For example, you could ask,

Games for the Classroom

"What time is 'The A-Team' on?", and "What time does 'The A-Team' finish?", before moving on to more complex reading comprehension questions such as, "What is the name of the actor who plays 'Mr.T' in 'The A-Team'?" Get the students to nominate a 'runner' from their team who runs and writes the answers on the board. You can even get them drawing clock faces as an answer, or writing the answer using the twenty four hour clock. Note: questions need not be 'A-Team'-based!

Board Game Boffins

As a project, get the students working in pairs or small groups to design a new board game. They have to form a games 'company', and then plan the concept and design of their game. After that they have to actually make a working prototype, which they test out, and which is then tested along with all the other ideas in a games tournament. Each company has to explain the reasons behind the design choices that they made in constructing their game. The students then all vote for their favourite games in categories such as: 'Most playable game', 'Game most likely to make a $million', 'Best design and construction', and so on. You could use the board game template on page 73 as a starting point.

Ten Things

Get your students to leave the building and go out in small groups or pairs with the task of writing down 'Ten things you can see at...' various places near to your school or college. For example, they could write down ten things you can see at... the leisure centre, the shopping centre, the sports stadium, the post office, the doctor's, the bus station, the railway station, the market, the funfair, and so on. Ask them to make sure that their spellings are correct before coming back to you with their list(s). Of course you could always make it 'Fifty things you can see at...' if your group are particularly gifted – or if you just want to get rid of them for the whole morning...! When they come back, discuss together what each group has found.

What Shops Sell What...?

This is a similar exercise to 'Ten Things', in that the students leave the classroom in pairs or small groups and go around town for a couple of hours. They have to write down the proper names of as many shops as they can, along with a brief description of what you can buy at that shop. For example, 'Marks and Spencer – clothes and food', 'Debenhams – clothes, gifts, and perfume', until they have a list of around twenty shops. When the students get back they could write sentences about the shops, for example, 'At Marks and Spencer you can buy clothes and food.' It motivates students to go into and look around shops that they may walk past every day but have never visited. You could always set the list of shops for your students to visit, ensuring a variety of types. Of course, it gives an opportunity to practise shopping vocab wherever you happen to be teaching.

Vocabulary Building

Name And Explain

This is a good game for practising spelling classroom words and getting students to talk about their immediate environment. Split the class into two groups and give each group a pack of sticky labels. Their task is to write labels and stick them on twenty different things in the classroom. Spellings must be correct, and at the end of the game students must give you a

Games for the Classroom

tour of their labelled items, explaining what each object is.

What Is It...?

Get the class into two teams. Take one student from each class out of the room, give them both a whiteboard pen (or chalk stick, or marker, etc.) and give them the name of a book, TV show (for example 'The A-Team'), film, or famous person. They have to run back into the room and draw clues on the board, while the other students try to guess the name that they have been given. They are not allowed to write any words. Students love this game, and it gets rather loud as the students get more involved. Make sure your students are aware of the cultural references that you want to give them. The game can be played just as well using vocab sets such as, furniture, food, animals, and so on.

What Am I...?

For this game you will need to put a sticker on the back of each student, with a noun written on it, for example, apple, chair, Wednesday, bathroom, or bottle of tomato ketchup. The students have to mingle with one another and ask questions to find out 'What am I...?' Students can only reply with either 'Yes' or 'No'. Once they have found out what they are, they report to you and tell you what they are and what questions they had to ask in order to work it out. They could then go and write down the different questions. This also works when you use celebrity names instead of nouns – as long as all the students are aware of exactly who all the celebrities are. You could also use specific vocab sets such as countries ('Am I north of the equator, or south?') or clothes ('Am I worn on the head?') The sky's the limit! Good for question forms and to get students talking.

Grammar Skills

A Capital Game

Write a load of nouns on the board, both common nouns and proper nouns, but don't use capital letters. Vary the list of words to suit the level of your group, so for an elementary class you could write something like: 'table, usa, book, house, garden, england, philip, the times, shirt, ice cream...' and so on. The students split into two groups and compete to be the first to write the list of words again, but this time putting capital letters on the proper nouns (in this example. 'USA, England, Philip, The Times').

Interesting Articles

Similar to 'A Capital Game', this involves writing plenty of different nouns on the board and getting the class – in two teams – to discuss and write down whether there should be 'a' or 'an' before each word. This is a quick and easy game – intended for elementary students really – that allows the students to identify and practise the grammar rule for indefinite articles. Make sure you throw a few proper nouns into the mix too, just to confuse them!

The Instant Story Generator

The whole group sits in a circle and decides on a few story keywords, for example, a place, a man's name, a woman's name, an object, and so on. Tell the students they are going to tell a story as a group. Each student can only contribute one word at a time, before the story

Games for the Classroom

moves on to the next person. If the story reaches a natural break the student whose turn it is next can say 'full stop' instead of carrying on. The story must include all the keywords that were agreed at the beginning. This is a great game for identifying sentence structure and bringing out grammar points, as well as letting the imagination run riot. A variation is to let each student contribute one sentence instead of just one word.

Action Games

Balloon Rodins

Split the class into small groups and give each one a large quantity of balloons and a roll of sticky tape. Their task is to create a fantastic balloon sculpture, which outshines those made by the other teams. After forty-five minutes or so the groups come together and look at all the sculptures. Each team has to describe what their sculpture represents – and is invited to elaborate on the principles of art that they have been influenced by... or not, as the case may be! Prepare yourselves for some 'explosive' balloon fun in this hilarious team-building and communicative activity! Note: this activity works just as well with modelling clay, or lots of old newspapers, instead of balloons.

Dead Heat

The class needs to be in groups of around eight people. Lay out a finish line at one end of the classroom with no desks or chairs in the way. The students stand in a line, as if about to start a race. On your signal they either run or walk towards the finishing line. However, all the students must cross the line at exactly the same time. A fun and energetic warmer which encourages students to talk to each other – particularly when they keep getting it wrong. Give your teams several attempts at this and they should get it in the end.

Get A Move On

Split the class into two teams. Set a starting line and a finishing line. This is basically a slow-walking race, where both teams are competing to be the last to cross the finishing line. The only proviso is that everyone in the race must keep moving forward – just very slowly. It's also good fun played with individuals in heats, building up to quarter-finals, semi-finals and a grand final. A fun team-building activity that will bring out the team spirit in your group.

Rhyming Words

International Phonetic Alphabet (IPA) - Vowels 1

ɪ / i / iː

ɪ	i	iː
vowel sound in 'f i sh'	*vowel sound in 'empt y'*	*vowel sound in 'f ee t'*

ɪ	i	iː
fish	empty	feet
dish	guilty	meet
wish	honesty	sheet
bid	rugby	feat
hid		heat
lid	lovely	neat
did	lily	treat
fill	juicy	Pete
hill	Lucy	mete
Jill		
still	smelly	deed
pill	jolly	need
bill	chilly	feed
Bill	frilly	speed
chill	Billy	
will	really	lead
kill		knead
	pretty	
pit	Betty	heal
it		steal
hit	hockey	deal
nit	jockey	
lit		peel
bit	movie	heel
spit		wheel
wit		
		speak
spin		leak
chin		
win		peek
tin		cheek
gin		
		dream
limb		team
		steam
list		
mist		seen
		been
missed		
		clean

Rhyming Words

International Phonetic Alphabet (IPA) - Vowels 2

æ / ɑː

æ

vowel sound in 'h a t'

hat	trap		
cat	flap		
fat	clap		
mat	tap		
spat	lap		
chat	cap		
gnat	nap		
splat	sap		
bat	rap		
brat	gap		
	yap		
Matt			
	channel		
can			
span	banner		
man	spanner		
woman	manner		
ban			
nan	tank		
tan	prank		
ran	spank		
fan	sank		
van	thank		
	bank		
land	shank		
hand	yank		
stand			
band	thanks		
and			
bandstand	back		
handstand	slack		
understand	hack		
brand	sack		
sand	shack		
	tack		
pal	knack		
gal			
map			
chap			

ɑː

vowel sound in 'c a r'

car	park
far	hark
bar	mark
tar	Mark
char	dark
par	
mar	barber
star	
guitar	harbour
Qatar	
	tart
are	cart
	smart
hurrah	art
shah	part
	dart
spa	mart
bra	
cha-cha	heart
ta	
pa	chance
	dance
ask	prance
task	lance
bask	advance
cask	stance
mask	
	father
branch	lather
	rather
hard	
card	
lard	
bard	
charred	
barred	
jarred	
bark	
lark	

Rhyming Words

International Phonetic Alphabet (IPA) - Vowels 3

ɒ / ɔː

ɒ

vowel sound in 'g o t'

ɔː

vowel sound in 'o r'

ɒ		ɔː	
got	sop	or	force
hot		for	
knot	box	nor	talk
not	fox		walk
shot	cox	pour	chalk
lot		four	
rot	off	your	hawk
plot	scoff		squawk
slot		poor	
trot	on	door	pork
clot	con		York
hotpot	Ron	pore	
cot		sore	board
jot	John	more	hoard
pot		bore	
sot	gone	yore	fought
tot		wore	nought
	from	core	ought
salt		fore	
halt	sock	gore	wart
Walt	knock	whore	
malt	rock	lore	form
	cock	tore	dorm
bolt	shock		
colt	dock	law	warm
dolt		jaw	
	wok	paw	warn
vault		straw	
fault	rob	draw	lawn
	Bob	raw	prawn
moult	sob	saw	sawn
	cob		pawn
stop	job	war	
top	lob		torn
chop	fob	oar	forlorn
hop	hob	hoar	
prop			
mop	odd	horse	
cop		Norse	
fop	wad		
pop		coarse	

Rhyming Words

International Phonetic Alphabet (IPA) - Vowels 4

ʊ / u / uː

ʊ	u	uː
*vowel sound in 'p **u** t'*	*vowel sound in 'sit **u** ate'*	*vowel sound in 't **oo**'*

ʊ

vowel sound in 'p u t'

put

soot
foot

book
hook
look
cook
crook
shook
brook
took
rook

wool

full
pull

good
hood

could
should
would

you'd

u

vowel sound in 'sit u ate'

situate

situation

educate

education

population
stimulation
calculation
simulation

populate
stimulate
calculate
simulate

uː

vowel sound in 't oo'

too

hue
cue

you

stew
crew

route

boot
loot

newt

cute

use
fuse

lose

bruise

June
dune

moon
soon

doom
room

cool
pool
school

group
soup

Rhyming Words

International Phonetic Alphabet (IPA) - Vowels 5

ə / ɜː

ə
vowel sound in 'a go'

ɜː
vowel sound in 'h e r'

ə		ɜː	
ago	unless	her	learn
adore		per	earn
about	president		turn
around	resident	stir	burn
annoy	confident	fir	
annul			stern
	somebody	whirr	fern
envelope	anybody		
	nobody	purr	worm
famous			
	London	cur	term
royal		fur	perm
loyal	woman		
		heard	firm
boil	family		
coil		herd	shirt
foil	motorway	nerd	skirt
	endless	bird	
banana	faithless		hurt
	harmless	stirred	
computer			pert
heater		purred	
under			first
user		word	thirst
teacher			
power		curd	worst
tower		turd	
brother			worse
mother		perch	
father			curse
sister		lurch	
daughter		church	verse
umbrella		birch	world
the		search	girl
hour		murder	furl
until		girder	hurl
			curl

Rhyming Words

International Phonetic Alphabet (IPA) - Vowels 6

e / ʌ

e

vowel sound in 't e n'

ʌ

vowel sound in 'u p'

e		ʌ	
ten	bet	up	tuck
hen	net	cup	sun
wren	jet	sup	fun
den	pet	pup	bun
men	set		shun
pen	vet	mud	stun
when		thud	
	debt	bud	gun
gem		stud	nun
hem	help	cud	pun
			run
fell	melt	blood	
tell	dwelt	flood	ton
bell	Celt		won
smell		rub	son
swell	tense	hub	
shell		club	one
dwell	whence	pub	done
spell		snub	
well	led	scrub	gull
	bed	cub	mull
gel	wed	tub	dull
	red		lull
spend	Ted	but	cull
mend		hut	
tend	head	shut	honey
lend	lead	cut	money
wend		nut	
bend	edge	rut	sunny
end	hedge		funny
trend	wedge	butt	bunny
	ledge	putt	runny
wreck		mutt	
speck	egg		sum
deck		luck	hum
neck	beg	duck	gum
peck	Meg	muck	chum
	peg	chuck	rum
get	keg	buck	
met	leg	puck	numb
let		suck	dumb

Rhyming Words

International Phonetic Alphabet (IPA) - Diphthongs 1

eɪ / əʊ

eɪ		əʊ	
*vowel sound in 'r **ai** n'*		*vowel sound in '**o** wn'*	
rain	vague	own	foam
train		grown	
Spain	nail	thrown	home
lain	sail	shown	dome
gain	hail	known	tome
main	pail		
chain	wail	bone	comb
fain	bail	cone	
pain	fail	lone	roamed
	jail	hone	
plane		scone	won't
Jane	whale	throne	don't
cane		clone	
sane	hale	phone	grow
Dane		stone	blow
	bait		know
reign		loan	row
feign	date	groan	show
	skate	moan	stow
mainly	gate		
plainly	late	cologne	woe
	fate		
waste	mate	sewn	hole
paste			whole
haste	weight	phoned	pole
taste	eight	cloned	mole
chaste		stoned	sole
baste	shame		
	lame	moaned	soul
base	came	loaned	
case	tame		soak
chase		owned	
	maim		poke
lace		hope	woke
face	take	mope	
pace	cake	cope	explode
race	sake		
mace	make	drove	load
place	wake	wove	
	lake		loaf
plague	shake	roam	oaf

Rhyming Words

International Phonetic Alphabet (IPA) - Diphthongs 2

aɪ / aʊ

aɪ

*vowel sound in 'b **y**'*

by	wild	cow	shout
spy		how	lout
sty	tiled	now	gout
shy	piled	wow	about
my		bow	pout
cry	styled	row	tout
try		brow	trout
	bite	allow	
buy	kite		doubt
guy	spite	bough	
	white	plough	clown
hi			town
pi	quite	bowel	brown
		towel	crown
lie	height	vowel	
tie		trowel	power
pie	flight		shower
	might	foul	tower
bye	night		bower
	sight	owl	cower
bike	tight	howl	
hike	right	cowl	sour
pike	bright	yowl	
like		scowl	pound
	byte	jowl	found
style		fowl	sound
	wine		wound
stile	shine	loud	hound
while	mine	proud	mound
mile	line	cloud	round
tile			around
pile	sign	crowd	
tied	time	bowed	
lied	lime	cowed	
	chime		
ride		house	
hide	rhyme	mouse	
		douse	
child	blind		
	find	out	

aʊ

*vowel sound in 'c **ow**'*

Rhyming Words

International Phonetic Alphabet (IPA) - Diphthongs 3

ɔɪ / ɪə

ɔɪ

*vowel sound in 't**oy**'*

toy	toiled
coy	coiled
boy	foiled
soy	spoiled
Roy	oiled
annoy	boiled
ploy	
joy	
Troy	
cloy	
destroy	
employ	
decoy	
deploy	
Illinois	
toyed	
annoyed	
employed	
deployed	
overjoyed	
enjoyed	
void	
avoid	
Freud	
boil	
soil	
toil	
coil	
foil	
spoil	
oil	
royal	
loyal	
soiled	

ɪə

*vowel sound in '**ea**r'*

ear	peered
year	steered
hear	cheered
appear	pioneered
dear	
clear	cleared
near	neared
tear	feared
gear	reared
fear	seared
disappear	
rear	tiered
sear	
	cheering
cheer	peering
beer	steering
leer	leering
sheer	pioneering
peer	jeering
deer	veering
steer	
engineer	searing
pioneer	fearing
volunteer	nearing
jeer	clearing
veer	
	shield
pier	wield
tier	field
chandelier	
cavalier	
here	
sphere	
mere	
we're	
Zaire	
pierce	

Rhyming Words

International Phonetic Alphabet (IPA) - Diphthongs 4

eə / ʊə

eə

vowel sound in 'air'

air	Claire	tour	luring
chair	millionaire		curing
hair	commissionaire	tourist	
fair			luxuriant
lair	square	tourism	
stair			curio
pair	aired	plural	
affair	chaired	rural	
despair	paired	mural	
flair	despaired		
éclair		neural	
unfair	pared		
	stared	usual	
there	fared	unusual	
where	bared		
	shared	neurotic	
their	prepared		
	declared	pure	
they're	dared	sure	
	flared	cure	
wear	cared	assure	
tear		lure	
bear	laird	allure	
mare		purely	
pare		surely	
stare			
rare		furious	
fare		curious	
Clare		luxurious	
share			
prepare		cured	
declare		lured	
dare		assured	
flare			
care		touring	
bare			
compare		alluring	
beware		assuring	
aware			

ʊə

vowel sound in 'tour'

Answers to Worksheets and Notes for Use

Grammar Skills

1 1. What's her name? – BE. 2. I don't know him. – DO, KNOW. 3. He went out. – GO. 4. Are you watching TV? – BE, WATCH. 5. I saw him yesterday. – SEE. 6. I have brought my friend. – HAVE, BRING. 7. They lost some money. – LOSE. 8. I don't like him. – DO, LIKE. 9. I have read your letter. – HAVE, READ. 10. We aren't learning much. – BE, LEARN. 11. I played on the computer. – PLAY. 12. I couldn't hear you. – CAN, HEAR. 13. Is it true? – BE. 14. Did she tell you my name? – DO, TELL. 15. That's her sister. – BE. 16. The time was about 8pm. – BE. 17. My arm really hurts. – HURT. 18. The children were laughing. – BE, LAUGH. 19. I washed my hands. – WASH. 20. We're seeing them later. – BE, SEE.

2 Note: the auxiliary verb is shown in **bold letters** and the main verb is underlined.
1. I went to the cinema yesterday. 2. I'**m** playing golf tomorrow. 3. We had an early lunch yesterday. 4. Her sister **is** going into hospital tomorrow. 5. What time **are** you getting up tomorrow? 6. I'**m** taking the car to the garage first thing tomorrow. 7. My brother moved house yesterday. 8. **Did** you see that new music shop in town yesterday? 9. I met Lisa and Isabella for a coffee yesterday. 10. He'**s** visiting his friend tomorrow afternoon. 11. There was a lot of noise outside yesterday. 12. We'**re** going swimming tomorrow morning. 13. **Are** you coming round tomorrow evening? 14. He **wasn't** at work yesterday afternoon because he went to hospital for an appointment. 15. John was in Birmingham all day yesterday for a meeting.

3 Note: the auxiliary verb is shown in **bold letters** and the main verb is underlined.
1. I gave them some homework yesterday. 2. I'**m** not going on holiday until tomorrow. 3. I missed the last bus yesterday, so I **had** to walk home. 4. It was cold yesterday, **wasn't** it? 5. Sally **is** getting her exam results tomorrow. 6. We packed our suitcases yesterday evening. 7. **Is** he still cooking lunch for his girlfriend and her family tomorrow? 8. Bob and Janet **are** coming round for a game of cards tomorrow night. 9. We'**re** flying to Spain tomorrow afternoon. 10. He'**s** playing football for a couple of hours tomorrow morning. 11. I saw your friend Ian in Sainsbury's yesterday. 12. I'**m** doing all my ironing tomorrow. 13. We both bought the same pair of shoes yesterday. 14. **Is** he **going** to tell you about the course tomorrow, or later on today? 15. Jen swam forty lengths of the pool yesterday.

4 1. I'm going to visit my sister **tomorrow** afternoon. 2. I went to my friend's house after work **yesterday** evening. 3. The cricket match started at 2pm **yesterday** afternoon. 4. I'm not going to play golf **tomorrow**. I had a good game **yesterday**. 5. We're going to buy a present for our friend **tomorrow**. 6. Rita told me **yesterday** that she's going to quit her job. 7. I watched that film you told me about **yesterday**. It was brilliant. 8. Are you going to get some more potatoes **tomorrow**? 9. She got up at quarter to ten **yesterday** morning! 10. She's going to get up earlier **tomorrow** morning. 11. I'm going to book a restaurant first thing **tomorrow**. 12. He was really tired **yesterday**, so he stayed at home all day. 13. I saw Ben **yesterday**. He's going to call you **tomorrow** night. 14. I finished reading that book you lent me **yesterday**. 15. Are you going to leave **tomorrow** or on Monday?

5 1. Phil's going to meet Abdul in town **tomorrow** afternoon. 2. Sereta didn't look very happy when I saw her **yesterday**. 3. We didn't get our exam results **yesterday** as promised. 4. Is James going to go on the trip **tomorrow**? 5. The builders finished early **yesterday**; at about 5 o'clock. 6. Sarah and Natalie are going to travel to London **tomorrow**. 7. Are you going to see that new Mel Gibson film when it comes out **tomorrow**?

Answers to Worksheets and Notes for Use

8. Did you watch the news **yesterday**? 9. You're going to feel tired **tomorrow** after all that exercise! 10. Did you send me an email **yesterday**? 11. I'm going to wash the car **tomorrow**. 12. Because my sister fell out with her best friend **yesterday**, they're not going to the gig **tomorrow** night. 13. Pete said he's going to walk to work **tomorrow**. 14. **Yesterday**, Olivier said that he isn't going to come to class next week because it's his granddad's birthday on Monday. 15. Were you at home **yesterday** evening?

6 1. Did you know I saw Steven **yesterday**? 2. What time will the lesson finish **tomorrow**? 3. I was going to ring you **yesterday**, but I didn't have time. 4. Jean caught the bus to work **yesterday** morning. 5. He would've liked to have seen you before you left **yesterday**, but never mind. 6. Both of us will be starting the new course **tomorrow** afternoon. 7. It will be almost impossible to finish this essay by **tomorrow**! 8. I was in Bristol **yesterday**, visiting my old friends Raphael and Henry. 9. Are you sure you had an appointment booked for **yesterday**? 10. Jamie said that he should have finished mending the fence by **tomorrow** afternoon. 11. I couldn't ask you about the report **yesterday** because you weren't in. 12. Samantha found out **yesterday** that her parents are splitting up. 13. The concert starts at seven **tomorrow**. 14. If I swim fifty lengths **tomorrow**, my teacher said she will enter me into the competition. 15. I couldn't ring you **yesterday** because I didn't have any credit on my phone.

7 1. The Prime Minister gave a long speech about the economy **yesterday**. It was pretty boring! 2. When I saw you **yesterday** I forgot to tell you that the conference won't be finishing until **tomorrow** night. 3. Sal should've told me **yesterday** that she won't be able to pay us **tomorrow**. 4. I could've had a lie in **yesterday**, if you weren't leaving so early. 5. Was it busy in town **yesterday**? 6. I'll be sorry to see you go when you leave **tomorrow**. 7. If I can get a day off work **tomorrow**, I'll be able to spend a bit of time with you. 8. If I could've bought you a birthday present **yesterday** I would've done. 9. We're going on holiday to Venice **tomorrow**. 10. I've never really liked Mexican food, but I really enjoyed the meal **yesterday**. 11. You must have rung the wrong number **yesterday**, because I was at home all morning. 12. Can you do the washing up that's been sitting here since **yesterday**, please? 13. We were gardening for about two hours **yesterday** morning. 14. Could I have a go on your new computer game when I come round **tomorrow**? 15. I think it should be quite sunny **tomorrow**.

8 Dear Ethel

I'm writing to tell you about something that happened yesterday. I **got** up at the usual time – about 10am – **had** a shower and **made** breakfast. I **ate** a big bowl of cereal and some toast and watched TV for a while. Then I **went** into the kitchen where I **heard** a funny noise. I **thought** it **came** from behind the cooker. I **got** my tool box and moved the cooker out of the way.

The noise **got** louder but I couldn't see anything. I **rang** my uncle to ask his advice. He **said** that he **thought** it could be a gas leak. When I **heard** this I just panicked! I **put** the phone down, **ran** outside, **got** in my car and **drove** to the local police station. I **told** them about my gas leak but the constable **lost** his patience with me. He **said** that I should have phoned the gas company. He **wrote** his report, then **rang** the gas company for me.

Answers to Worksheets and Notes for Use

Then I remembered that my house doesn't have gas – only electricity! I **felt** really stupid and **knew** that the constable would be angry with me for wasting his time, so I **ran** out of the police station while he **was** still on the phone. I **went** home to try to find out what the noise **was**. On the way I **bought** a newspaper and I **read** about an escaped llama that **broke** out of the city safari park last Wednesday.

When I **got** home I **put** my key in the door, turned it, **went** inside and straight away **heard** that funny noise again. I **held** my breath and opened the door slowly. Guess what? I **found** the llama hiding in my cupboard! I **let** him stay and he **slept** in my garden last night. The snoring **was** so loud! This morning I **took** him back to the safari park. They **were** really pleased to see him again and **gave** me a reward of £50!

Hope you are well. Write soon and let me know how you are. Your friend, Alan

9 & 10 Print each page onto card. Cut up the pieces and then ask your students to match the first part of the sentence with the second part.

11 1. This is my pen _____. 2. There are two pens on the table. 3. These pens are on the table. 4. There are a few pens on the table. 5. There is one pen _____ on the table. 6. There are lots of pens on the table. 7. There are some big pens on the table 8. There is a pen _____ on the table. 9. There is a big pen _____ on the table. 10. This is his pen _____. 11. There is a box of pens on the table. 12. That pen _____ is on the table. 13. Why are those pens on the table? 14. These are the only pens on the table. 15. There is a large quantity of pens on the table.

12 1. There are some pens on the table. 2. There are not many pens on the table. 3. This pen _____ is on the table. 4. There is not a single pen _____ on the table. 5. There are hardly any pens on the table. 6. Those pens are on the table. 7. This is their pen _____. 8. There are several pens on the table. 9. There are twenty three pens on the table. 10. This is the last pen _____. 11. This is the only pen _____. 12. There is a new pen _____ on the table. 13. There is a packet of pens on the table. 14. There is another pen _____ on the table. 15. There aren't any pens on the table.

13-14 Note: answers will vary. The key point is that the determiner and noun must agree in each answer. Here are some suggestions:

13 1. a green bag. 2. some big tables. 3. a beautiful picture. 4. ten long dresses. 5. the new black trousers. 6. an uncooked egg. 7. an annoying person. 8. some nice people. 9. some fresh sandwiches. 10. a good programme. 11. an interesting journey. 12. a few young men. 13. a lot of big problems. 14. the left-hand side. 15. an old suitcase.

14 1. a lot of noise. 2. our two children. 3. some great offers. 4. this tall building. 5. the new magazines. 6. a stupid mistake. 7. each piece of paper. 8. some fast cars. 9. all the right people. 10. a new team leader. 11. a complete mess. 12. an early morning. 13. fewer problems. 14. a hot cup of coffee. 15. some terrible reviews.

15

a	book	✓	**his**	book	✓
	books	x		books	✓
	umbrella	x		umbrella	✓
	umbrellas	x		umbrellas	✓
	London	x		London	x

Answers to Worksheets and Notes for Use

an	book	x		book	✓
	books	x		books	x
	umbrella	✓	**this**	umbrella	✓
	umbrellas	x		umbrellas	x
	London	x		London	x
the	book	✓		book?	✓
	books	✓		books?	✓
	umbrella	✓	**which**	umbrella?	✓
	umbrellas	✓		umbrellas?	✓
	London	x		London?	x
some	book	x		book	x
	books	✓		books	✓
	umbrella	x	**those**	umbrella	x
	umbrellas	✓		umbrellas	✓
	London	x		London	x

Vocabulary Skills

16   1. adventure. 2. amazement. 3. ability. 4. anger. 5. anxiety. 6. beauty. 7. bravery. 8. chaos. 9. compassion. 10. contentment. 11. confidence. 12. courage. 13. curiosity. 14. deceit. 15. democracy. 16. determination. 17. disappointment. 18. education. 19. egotism. 20. energy.

17   1. enthusiasm. 2. evil. 3. excitement. 4. faithfulness. 5. fear. 6. friendliness. 7. generosity. 8. goodness. 9. graciousness. 10. happiness. 11. homelessness. 12. humour. 13. imagination. 14. inflation. 15. intelligence. 16. jealousy. 17. joy. 18. kindness. 19. loyalty. 20. luck.

18   1. e) 2. a) 3. c) 4. b) 5. d) 6. j) 7. f) 8. g) 9. i) 10. h)

19   1. b) 2. c) 3. g) 4. e) 5. a) 6. i) 7. f) 8. d) 9. j) 10. h)

20   1. e) 2. d) 3. g) 4. f) 5. b) 6. i) 7. a) 8. h) 9. c) 10. j)

21   1. j) 2. e) 3. b) 4. d) 5. a) 6. g) 7. h) 8. c) 9. i) 10. f)

22   1. tub. 2. can. 3. packet. 4. ball. 5. tube. 6. book. 7. jar. 8. half. 9. cup. 10. plate. 11. bowl. 12. dozen. 13. piece. 14. pat. 15. bottle.

23   Students' answers will vary. Here are some suggestions: 1. soap. 2. tea. 3. water. 4. bread. 5. toast. 6. beer. 7. milk. 8. lemonade. 9. crisps. 10. biscuits. 11. string. 12. jam. 13. people. 14. cakes. 15. ham. 16. cream. 17. gloves. 18. children. 19. coins. 20. chocolate. 21. cereal. 22. flowers. 23. sand. 24. washing powder. 25. matches. 26. cola. 27. petrol. 28. water. 29. ale. 30. milk. 31. petrol. 32. clothes. 33. cards. 34. rain. 35. ink. 36. beans.

24   Here are some examples of quantity words that go well with these shopping words.

Answers to Worksheets and Notes for Use

Can you think of any more? 1. a packet of crisps. 2. a loaf of bread. 3. a bar of chocolate. 4. a carton of orange juice. 5. a tub of ice cream. 6. a packet of chewing gum. 7. a packet of sandwiches. 8. a bottle of milk. 9. a jar of jam. 10. a slice of cake. 11. a bottle of lemonade. 12. a piece of cheese. 13. a bag of lettuce. 14. a plate of fish. 15. a tin of baked beans.

25   **Tim:** nephew, sister-in-law, ex-wife, partner, single. **Sally:** boyfriend, cousin, godson, godmother, divorced.

26   **Peter:** children, gay, widower, engaged, great-grandfather. **Ellie:** widow, ex-husband, girlfriend, fiancée, dysfunctional.

27   1. sister. 2. mother/mum. 3. daughter-in-law. 4. brother. 5. niece. 6. husband. 7. sister-in-law. 8. partner. 9. ex-husband. 10. grandmother/grandma. 11. aunt. 12. grandfather/granddad. 13. uncle. 14. son. 15. grandson. 16. wife. 17. daughter. 18. cousin. 19. brother-in-law. 20. father/dad.

28   Answers will vary. Some suggested answers are: 1. in. 2. jam. 3. real. 4. Cairo. 5. nearly. 6. equator. 7. tomorrow. 8. beautiful.

29   1. undercover. 2. outgoing. 3. genuine. 4. diverse. 5. pleased. 6. concealed. 7. green. 8. immature. 9. happy. 10. prized. 11. baffling. 12. unsatisfactory. 13. loose. 14. good-looking. 15. indefatigable.

30   1. unintentional. 2. gifted. 3. specialised. 4. uninteresting. 5. articulate. 6. authentic. 7. old. 8. trustworthy. 9. pleasant. 10. terrible. 11. scary. 12. modern. 13. chilly. 14. well-built. 15. unworkable.

31   1. beau. 2. berth. 3. laze. 4. feint. 5. inn. 6. yoke. 7. teem. 8. pi. 9. cord. 10. meter. 11. isle/aisle. 12. fir. 13. bury. 14. draught. 15. whet.

32   1. gait. 2. hart. 3. dessert. 4. lieu. 5. bored. 6. flare. 7. wail. 8. suite. 9. beet. 10. saw. 11. Yule. 12. wile. 13. higher. 14. byte. 15. ail.

34   1. h) 2. l) 3. j) 4. i) 5. o) 6. d) 7. m) 8. c) 9. f) 10. a) 11. n) 12. e) 13. g) 14. b) 15. k)

35   Answers will vary. Here are some suggestions: 1. It's very foggy. 2. It's sunny and warm. 3. It's very windy. 4. It's foggy or misty. 5. It's becoming windy. 6. It's raining lightly. 7. The snow has almost melted. 8. It's a lightning storm. 9. It might start raining. 10. It's cold. 11. It's very sunny. 12. It's very cold. 13. It's hot. 14. It has started snowing (at Christmas time). 15. It's very hot.

36   Answers will vary. Here are some suggestions: 1. It's cloudy. 2. It's cold. 3. It is, or has been, snowing heavily. 4. It's raining hard. 5. It's a lightning storm. 6. It's raining. 7. It's thundering. 8. It's fine. 9. It looks like it might be cold. 10. It's warm. 11. It's icy and cold. 12. It's hot. 13. It's cloudy. 14. It's cold and frosty. 15. It's very hot.

Spelling Skills

38   holiday, August, family; staying, campsite; brother, coming, because; leave, early, o'clock; hundred, caravans; forward, going, swimming, diving; should, really, holiday.

Answers to Worksheets and Notes for Use

39 sauce, tomato, mushroom; ice cream, vanilla, strawberry; oranges, apples; sausages, Saturday; Breakfast, muesli; chocolate cake, Friday; Coffee, sugar, pineapple squash; vegetables, potatoes, carrots.

40 "To get to the bank you <u>need</u> to <u>turn</u> left here then <u>walk</u> for about 200 <u>metres</u>. Turn right onto Stockley <u>Street</u> and <u>you'll</u> see the park on your left. Walk <u>past</u> the main <u>entrance</u> to the park and turn <u>right</u> into Bromley <u>Avenue</u>. The bank is <u>about</u> 100 <u>metres</u> down Bromley Avenue. <u>It's</u> <u>opposite</u> the post <u>office</u>. It's not far from here – <u>probably</u> about 15 <u>minutes</u> if you walk <u>quickly</u>. <u>You'd</u> better hurry as I think it closes at five <u>o'clock</u>."

41 "I left <u>school</u> nearly <u>fifteen</u> years ago. My <u>favourite</u> subjects <u>were</u> English, <u>French</u> and History. I enjoyed French <u>because</u> it was <u>interesting</u> learning to speak a <u>different</u> <u>language</u> and I had a good <u>teacher</u>. I didn't like Science or Maths because they were a bit harder and I <u>didn't</u> like the teachers much. I'll <u>never</u> forget when our <u>class</u> went on a trip to <u>France</u>. We stayed in Paris for <u>four</u> <u>nights</u>. It was the <u>first</u> time I'd been <u>abroad</u>. My <u>friends</u> and I had so <u>much</u> fun!"

42

25th September 2004
Cardiff, UK

Dear Aunt Monica

Thank you very much for your letter. It was great to get a letter from you. I am really enjoying university life. I have made some good friends already – especially Helen and Marcus. Helen is from Manchester and Marcus comes from Liverpool. His accent is really weird.

Yesterday we went to Cardiff to do some shopping. Everything is much more expensive than back at home. I miss Jamaica and of course I miss you and my naughty little brothers. Cardiff is a big city – the capital city of Wales. Wales is next to England and a separate country, but they are both part of the UK. It's confusing, isn't it?

My course is very interesting. I am learning so much about the environment of this country. My teachers are good, except I wish they would speak more slowly some of the time. I can't always hear everything that they are saying. That's why I'm using a small tape recorder to record every lecture. Then I can listen to it in my room as I study. It really helps.

Thanks for asking about all my boyfriends! No, I haven't met anyone yet. I'm here to learn about the environment and practise my English, rather than go out drinking in pubs and clubs with boys every night! I hope that I will find someone who shares my interests. Until that time you will have to make do with me being a single girl!

With lots of love to you and my darling brothers Roger and Paul, and all my family and friends there. I will see you very soon. Hope I will hear from you soon too.

Your loving niece

Sandy x x x x

Answers to Worksheets and Notes for Use

43 embarrass, coming, believe, analyse, curriculum; necessarily, calendar, coolly, eighth, February; manoeuvre, disappear, fifteen, weird, referral.

44 receipt, separate, pigeon, fulfil, mischief; belief, hundred, Caribbean, wholly, attached; niece, rhythm, twelfth, occurrence, sergeant.

45 generally, achievement, exercise, commission, forty; separation, puerile, parallel, exaggerate, liaison; appetite, dissatisfied, necessary, quandary, succeeded.

46 beginning, millennium, immediately, definitely, vegetable; innocuous, raspberry, precede, besiege, address; supersede, drunkenness, millionaire, incidentally, cemetery.

47 1. THE LONDON EYE. 2. BUCKINGHAM PALACE. 3. HOUSES OF PARLIAMENT. 4. BIG BEN. 5. ST PAUL'S CATHEDRAL. 6. LONDON BRIDGE. 7. WATERLOO BRIDGE. 8. HARRODS. 9. OXFORD STREET. 10. PICCADILLY CIRCUS. 11. TRAFALGAR SQUARE. 12. HYDE PARK. 13. ST JAMES'S PARK. 14. NATIONAL THEATRE. 15. NATIONAL PORTRAIT GALLERY. 16. COVENT GARDEN. 17. ROYAL FESTIVAL HALL. 18. GLOBE THEATRE. 19. NELSON'S COLUMN. 20. LEICESTER SQUARE.

Reading Skills

48 1. b) Terrible! 2. d) I don't think so. 3. d) Have a break. 4. d) Not really. 5. b) Not much. 6. c) On the table. 7. b) About eight o'clock. 8. d) No, I didn't know. 9. c) Thanks. 10. b) Is there?

49 1. c) Sometime next summer. 2. d) Fine. 3. a) It's chucking it down. 4. b) About half of it. 5. c) If she wants. 6. b) Really? 7. a) Oh. Do you know where? 8. d) Here you are. 9. c) How do you know? 10. b) Only by mistake.

50 1. c) We'd better hurry then. 2. b) I'm not sure. 3. b) Two years ago. 4. a) Oh dear. 5. d) Hi. 6. d) I'm alright, thanks. 7. a) Turn left and go through the double doors. 8. b) No, she's upstairs in a meeting. 9. d) See you. 10. d) The week after next.

51 1. b) Egg and chips. 2. c) Quarter past. 3. a) It's his own fault. 4. c) That's fifty six pence, please. 5. d) No, we haven't decided yet. 6. a) How old are you? 7. c) It varies. 8. a) Why not? 9. d) They're on the kitchen table. 10. a) Oh no!

52 1. c) Nearly eighteen 2. a) You'll have to find a new one. 3. d) No, it's not! 4. b) Yes, I did. 5. d) Housing, please. 6. b) Why were you early? 7. c) rach990@purlandtraining.com. 8. d) Yes, of course. 9. a) You poor thing! 10. d) Some of it.

53-62 Note: as well as being used as reading comprehension tests, these worksheets could also be used with learners as oral tests. **Method:** read the text aloud and ask learners to make notes from what they hear. They should then compare their notes with a partner or the whole group. Read the text again and learners should check their notes and refine them, before comparing them again with their partner or group when you finish reading. You could then either ask the questions verbally or

Answers to Worksheets and Notes for Use

give learners a photocopy of the questions only. Check feedback with the whole group at the end of the activity. You could give learners a copy of the initial text for reference. With lower level groups you could do the reading and note-taking step a third time.

53 1. Bob Hunter. 2. Forty years old. 3. Derby. 4. Yes. 5. Three. 6. Linda. 7. She's an artist. 8. Richard. 9. Engineering. 10. Fourteen years old. 11. Derby Grammar School. 12. Sally. 13. Twelve years old. 14. Horse-riding and cycling. 15. He is an accountant. 16. Toyota. 17. Yes. 18. He plays golf. 19. Mickleover Golf Club. 20. When he was eleven years old.

54 1. Samantha. 2. One day last month. 3. Home. 4. Trying to break into a car. 5. "Get lost!" 6. The shop's owner. 7. About ten minutes later. 8. No, a policewoman did. 9. Dark blue. 10. Ford Focus. 11. The right hand side. 12. TR03 RMN8. 13. Tall. 14. A blue denim jacket and black jeans. 15. A little shaken. 16. A few days later. 17. Newcastle. 18. It was returned to its owner. 19. No. 20. The text doesn't tell us this.

55 1. Next summer. 2. Joanna and Ling. 3. False – she went to southern Spain. 4. Three. 5. It was quite expensive. 6. False – they all got great suntans. 7. Greece. 8. Her parents. 9. An adventure holiday. 10. Africa. 11. She isn't sure whether she wants to go. 12. Because they would learn about the world around them and see some wild animals. 13. Relaxing on a beach. 14. Elephants and zebras. 15. Amazing experiences. 16. By next Monday at the latest. 17. £1,400. 18. Portugal. 19. & 20. Learners can discuss their answers to these questions.

56 1. Serena. 2. Devon, UK. 3. At about 8.30am. 4. Cereal. 5. A fry-up (cooked breakfast). 6. George. 7. The washing up. 8. A Telegraph. 9. Because he likes doing the crossword. 10. A couple of hours. 11. A nice restaurant on the coast. 12. A fresh seafood dish. 13. Relax for a while and be alone. 14. Either explore the town, or go to the beach for a couple of hours. 15. At about 5 o'clock. 16. Go out for a drink or go to the theatre. 17. A comedy. 18. Go straight to bed. 19. & 20. Learners can discuss their answers to these questions.

57 1. Emma Heath. 2. She is looking for a new job. 3. She is a clerk at a solicitor's. 4. Administrator. 5. Blame, Payne and Co. 6. About two years. 7. There doesn't seem to be any chance of promotion, and she is moving to Leicester. 8. Leicester. 9. 23 Terraced Walk, Derby, DE23 3GP. 10. No. She will be renting. 11. 8 Cedars Lane, Swinscote, Derby, DE40 9UR. 12. After the 30th of the month. 13. 0 + 7 + 9 + 4 = 20. 14. After six o'clock pm. 15. By at least £2000, or more. 16. A document used to give potential employers information about a job applicant. 17. Curriculum Vitae. 18. She doesn't know. 19. & 20. Learners can discuss their answers to these questions.

58 1. Tim has £1.47. 2. John has £7.17. 3. Clare has £12.51. 4. Lisa doesn't have any money. 5. Jalal has £6.75. 6. Jalal's brother has 75p. 7. Keith has 58p. 8. Kathy has £50.68. 9. Laurie doesn't have any money. 10. Ruby has £5.

59 1. Joe's birthday is on 23rd May. 2. Colette's birthday is on 25th May. 3. Conor's birthday is on 17th May. 4. Laura's birthday is on 22nd December. 5. May's birthday is on 19th August. 6. Sarah's birthday is on 17th September. 7. Leanne's birthday is on 13th February. 8. Leanne's husband's birthday is on 23rd August. 9. Tom's birthday is

Answers to Worksheets and Notes for Use

on 13th June. 10. Mohammed's birthday is on 11th February.

60 1. Sian. 2. Khalid. 3. From Derby to Edinburgh. 4. Four hours and twenty-three minutes. 5. Four hours and seven minutes. 6. One. 7. Two hours and thirty-six minutes. 8. Darlington. 9. Two hours. 10. The train to Newcastle is run by Virgin Trains. 11. Two twenty one pm, or, twenty one minutes past two in the afternoon. 12. GNER. 13. You could fly from Nottingham East Midlands Airport. It takes about an hour. 14. Two thirty pm, or half past two in the afternoon. 15. Three: Sian, her sister and her sister's friend. 16. About half past eight. 17. Michelle. 18. Next Tuesday. 19. Tomorrow night after work – any time after about quarter past six. 20. 08457 484950.

61 1. Spain. 2. Kamal was quiet and Hélène was loud. 3. From Kirkuk in Iraq. 4. Hélène. 5. Carolina. She's two years younger than Mohammad, who is 30. 6. Charlotte. 7. 24. 8. Yui-Gui. 9. There were 3 female students and 4 male students. 10. Eritrea. 11. Beijing. 12. Patrick is the oldest and Alexandre is the youngest. 13. 38. 14. Patrick. 15. Charlotte. 16. Carolina and Alexandre. 17. Two. 18. Kamal. 19. Patrick. 20. 35 (35.3).

62 1. 1.30am. 2. 3.30am. 3. 1.05am. 4. 3.45pm. 5. 2.44am. 6. 11.15am. 7. 2.15pm. 8. 5.30pm. 9. 4.45pm. 10. 7.44am. 11. Marco. 12. 8.30am. 13. His flatmate, Gordon. 14. Toronto, Canada. 15. Because Graham's phone call woke up the whole family at 2.44am.

Speaking & Listening Skills

63 This template can be used in various ways to create many different class surveys. One method is for students to write down a question such as, 'Which foods do you like?' They then write up to eight different options in separate boxes along the top row, for example: 'pasta, fish and chips, curry, lamb, chocolate biscuits, fruit, jacket potatoes, ice cream'. They interview different members of the class, writing the name of each person they ask in a separate box in the left-hand column. Students put a tick or a cross in the box to indicate whether their interviewee likes (tick) or dislikes (cross) each option.

Research Skills

66 1. London. 2. Green. 3. For example: in, on, above, below, under. 4. For example: a dentist, a receptionist, a drill, a waiting room, a dentist's chair. 5. Buy a ticket and catch a train. 6. For example: apple, arm, ankle, animal, arch. 7. For example: Trent, Tyne, Mersey. 8. Sunday (or you could accept Monday). 9. 75 years old. 10. A horse. 11. For example: the living room. 12. £7.00. 13. It's an odd number. 14. Eight forty five pm. 15. One thousand, two hundred and thirty four. 16. He was Prime Minister of the UK from 1990-1997. 17. There are five – A, E, I, O and U. 18. Accommodation. 19. Small. 20. Answers will vary.

67 1. Paris. 2. Answers will vary. 3. For example: football, cricket, rugby, swimming, baseball. 4. For example: an oven, a fridge, a sideboard, some washing-up liquid, a saucepan. 5. Buy petrol. 6. For example: orange, olive, octopus, ocean, owner.

Answers to Worksheets and Notes for Use

7. River Thames. 8. October. 9. 43 years old. 10. For example: a zebra. 11. For example: bedroom. 12. £20.15. 13. It's an even number. 14. Three eighteen am. 15. One hundred and ninety two. 16. Gordon Brown MP (as at October 2004). 17. 168. 18. Proposition. 19. Near. 20. Answers will vary.

69 airport, blood, carrot, dove, England, friend, go, hat, Ireland, January, kite, lorry, money, never, orange, picture, question, rose, shed, trainer, unhappy/upset, vinegar, wine, xylophone, yellow, zip.

70 alien, bank, cat, Dover, EastEnders, Friday, gentle, heart, Italy, jeans, kettle, loan, meat, near, one, present, queue, red, sheep, title, ugly, Venice, winter, x-factor, yes, zebra.

71 Antarctica, bells, castle, dog, ears, free, golf, hospital, idiot, joke, kennel, languages, Monopoly, nest, omelette, pockets, Quebec, ruler, strong, tears, umbrella, velvet, weather, x-ray, year, zero.

72 This is a blank template which learners can use to make their own wordsearches. **Method:** write twenty words that are related in some way, for example, languages, colours or film stars. Make sure that all of the spellings are correct. Then, write the words in the grid, with one letter in each space. Words can go horizontally, vertically, diagonally, right way up, or wrong way up – it doesn't matter. When all the words are in the grid, fill in the remaining squares with random letters of the alphabet, to 'hide' the words that you have added. Tip: make your wordsearch more difficult by adding 'red herrings'. For example, if one of your words is 'YELLOW', you could add 'YELL' or 'YELLO' as you fill up the remaining spaces.

73 This worksheet works best when photocopied and enlarged to at least A3 size. Split your students into small groups and ask them to design a board game (see 'Board Game Boffins' – page 89).

74 The real place names are: Bride – Isle of Man, Bottoms – West Yorkshire, Evenjobb – Powys, Macduff – Aberdeenshire, Idle – West Yorkshire, St Bees – Cumbria, Yelling – Cambridgeshire, Bell o' th' Hill – Cheshire, Red Ball – Somerset, Anna Valley – Hampshire.

75 All of the place names are real! Kelly – Devon, London Apprentice – Cornwall, Beer – Devon, Stanley Crook – Durham, Belchford – Lincolnshire, Much Hoole – Lancashire, Norton-Juxta-Twycross – Leicestershire, Bishop's Itchington – Warwickshire, Clopton Corner – Suffolk, Read – Lancashire, Watermillock – Cumbria, Little Wilbraham – Cambridgeshire, Weston-under-Lizard – Staffordshire, Trumpet – Herefordshire, Inkpen – Berkshire, River – West Sussex, Pratt's Bottom – Greater London, Homer – Shropshire, Rose – Pembrokeshire, Shilbottle – Northumberland.

76 1. c) 2. i) 3. f) 4. a) 5. h) 6. b) 7. k) 8. m) 9. e) 10. g) 11. d) 12. n) 13. o) 14. j) 15. l)

77 1. g) 2. e) 3. b) 4. f) 5. h) 6. d) 7. k) 8. m) 9. j) 10. n) 11. o) 12. a) 13. i) 14. c) 15. l)

78 1. Portsmouth, England. 2. 7th February 1812. 3. John and Elizabeth Dickens. 4. Chatham school, Kent, and Wellington House Academy, London. 5. At Warren's Blacking Factory – a shoe-blacking warehouse. 6. A solicitor's clerk and a reporter on

Answers to Worksheets and Notes for Use

Commons (Parliamentary) debates. 7. Boz. 8. Maria Beadnell. 9. Dora Spenlow in David Copperfield. 10. Catherine Hogarth. 11. 1836. 12. Choose from: Charles, Mary, Kate, Walter, Francis, Alfred, Sydney, Henry, Dora, and Edward. 13. Among the most well known are: Great Expectations, Bleak House, David Copperfield, Oliver Twist, The Pickwick Papers, Our Mutual Friend, and Nicholas Nickleby. 14. Nicholas Nickleby. 15. Ebeneezer Scrooge in A Christmas Carol. 16. 1851. 17. Gad's Hill Place. 18. 1858. 19. Ellen Ternan. 20. 9th June 1870 at Gad's Hill Place.

79 Answers will vary. Here are some suggestions: **A** – An aggressive argument. **B** – Another name for your navel. **C** – A silly mistake. **D** – A complete mess; plans gone wrong. **E** – Very easy; a child could do it. **F** – What you get when you steal. **G** – A racehorse. **H** – Very big. **I** – Too sentimental; makes you cringe. **J** – Cockney rhyming slang for 'piano'. **K** – A punch in the mouth from somebody's fist. **L** – A man who is often seen at trendy wine bars. **M** – Formal evening dress for men.

80 Answers will vary. Here are some suggestions: **N** – good; works well; desirable. **O** – enthusiasm; effort. **P** – very ugly. **Q** – a doctor with a poor reputation. **R** – a vehicle that needs a lot of work. **S** – the roll of fat around a fat person's waist. **T** – 'bye; see ya (informal goodbye). **U** – to throw up; vomit. **V** – to leave quickly. **W** – something you can't remember. **X** – Christmas. **Y** – a young, wealthy professional person. **Z** – someone whose wealth seems to have no limits.

81 1. i) 2. a) 3. j) 4. k) 5. g) 6. e) 7. d) 8. f) 9. b) 10. m) 11. o) 12. h) 13. l) 14. c) 15. n)

82 1. j) 2. l) 3. e) 4. g) 5. n) 6. k) 7. c) 8. o) 9. b) 10. a) 11. f) 12. d) 13. i) 14. h) 15. m)

83 1. G. 2. H. 3. C. 4. E. 5. D. 6. K. 7. I. 8. F. 9. L. 10. A. 11. J. 12. B.

84 Note: some dates are the same every year while others vary from year to year:

New Year's Day is on 1st January. It's the first day of the year and a public holiday. **St Valentine's Day** is on 14th February. We send cards and gifts to our loved ones. **St David's Day** is on 1st March. St David is the Patron Saint of Wales. **Pancake Day (Shrove Tuesday)** is usually in early March, on a Tuesday. It's the day before the Christian period of Lent begins. **St Patrick's Day** is on 17th March. St Patrick is the Patron Saint of Ireland. **Mother's Day** is usually in March, on a Sunday. We give cards and gifts to our mums. **British Summer Time** usually starts in March, on a Sunday. Our clocks go forward one hour, so we lose an hour's sleep. How annoying! **Good Friday** is in either March or April. Christians remember the death of Jesus Christ. It is a public holiday in the UK. **Easter Sunday** comes two days after Good Friday. Christians remember the resurrection of Jesus Christ. **Easter Monday Bank Holiday** occurs the day after Easter Sunday. A 'bank holiday' means it is a public holiday. **St George's Day** is on 23rd April. St George is the Patron Saint of England. **May Day Bank Holiday** is on the first Monday in May. **Spring Bank Holiday** is on the last Monday in May. **Father's Day** is usually in mid-June, on a Sunday. We give cards and gifts to our dads. The **Longest Day (Summer Solstice)** is usually in the third week of June. On the Longest Day we have the maximum number of hours of daylight. After today the hours of daylight per day go down each day, until we reach the Shortest Day in the third week of December. **August Bank Holiday** is on the last Monday in August. **British Summer Time** usually ends in October, on a Sunday. Our clocks go back one hour so we get an extra hour in bed (on this day only!).

Answers to Worksheets and Notes for Use

Hallowe'en is on 31st October. Children celebrate all things scary and spooky. **Bonfire Night** is on 5th November. We remember Guy Fawkes and his failed gunpowder plot to blow up the British Parliament and kill King James I in 1605. **Remembrance Sunday** is on the second Sunday in November. We remember all the servicemen and women who have died in wars and conflicts around the globe. The **Shortest Day (Winter Solstice)** is usually in the third week of December. On the Shortest Day we have the least number of hours of daylight. After today the hours of daylight per day increase each day, until we reach the Longest Day in the third week of June. **Christmas Eve** is on 24th December. The day before the Christian festival of Christmas. **Christmas Day** is on 25th December. Christians celebrate the birth of Jesus Christ. It is a public holiday in the UK. **Boxing Day** is on 26th December. It is a public holiday in the UK. **New Year's Eve** is on 31st December. We celebrate the year that has passed and look forward to the coming new year.

85 Bingo is a popular game in the UK, played by thousands of people every week, often for large cash prizes. I'm not suggesting you start giving away millions in class, but students always have a lot of fun competing for more modest prizes, such as chocolate bars and so on! **Method:** copy the worksheets and cut up the bingo cards. Give one to each student and ask them to write down a random selection of fifteen numbers between 1-90 – one in each of the blank spaces. You could play bingo by either using a machine or computer software program that can generate numbers randomly, or you could think of a random set of numbers yourself. If you do the latter, make sure you write down the numbers that you have read out, so that you can check the winning student's bingo card for accuracy. Give prizes for the first student to complete any line, then the first student to complete their game board. If the same person wins both times, keep playing and award the remaining prize to whoever finishes next.

www.ingramcontent.com/pod-product-compliance
Lightning Source LLC
Chambersburg PA
CBHW081116080526
44587CB00021B/3621